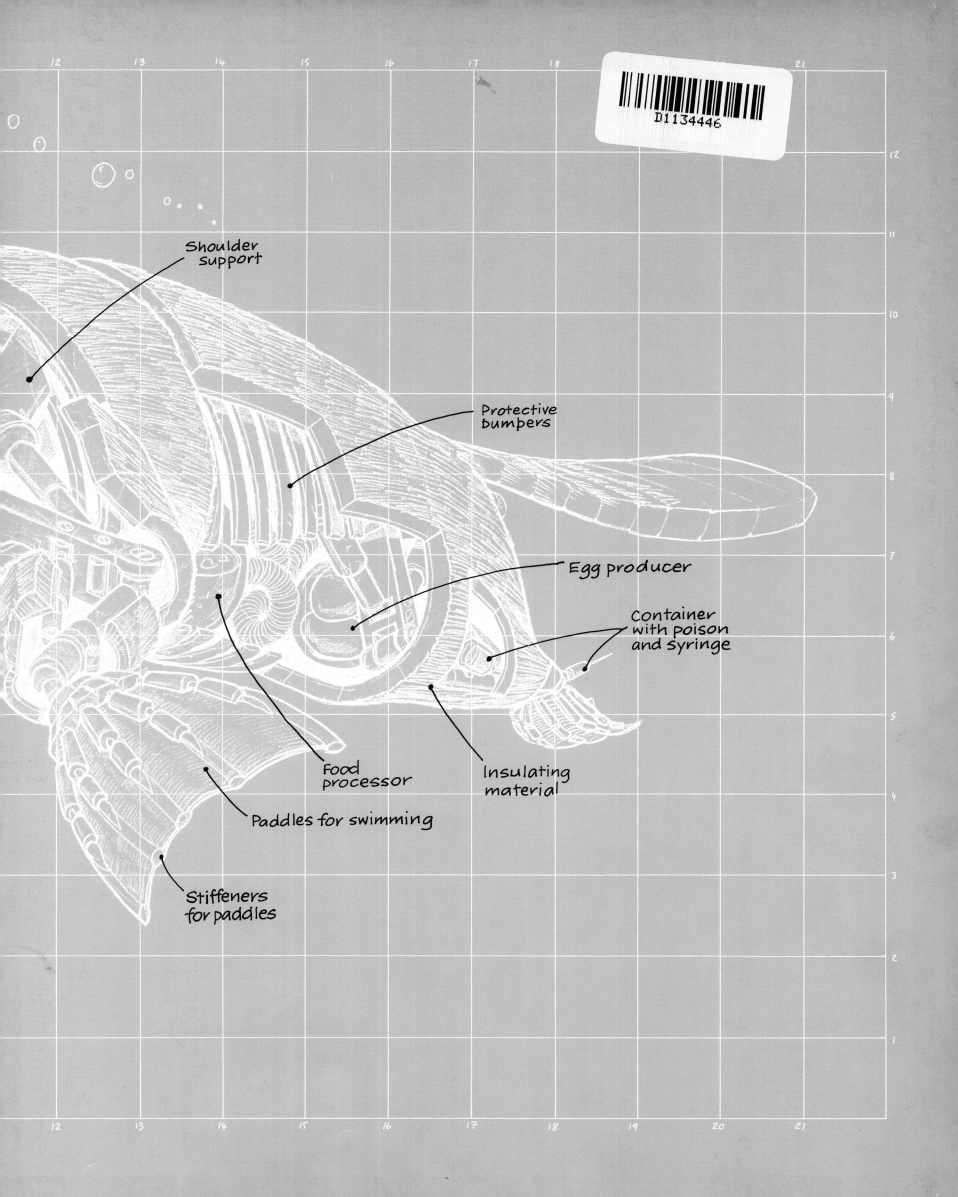

Shoulder
support

Protective
bumpers

Egg producer

Container
with poison
and syringe

Food
processor

Insulating
material

Paddles for swimming

Stiffeners
for paddles

A Marshall Edition
Conceived, edited and designed by Marshall Editions,
170 Piccadilly, London W1V 9DD

First published in Great Britain in 1994 by Hamlyn Children's Books,
an imprint of Reed Children's Books,
Michelin House, 81 Fulham Road, London SW3 6RB,
and Auckland, Melbourne, Singapore and Toronto.

ISBN 0 600 58497 6

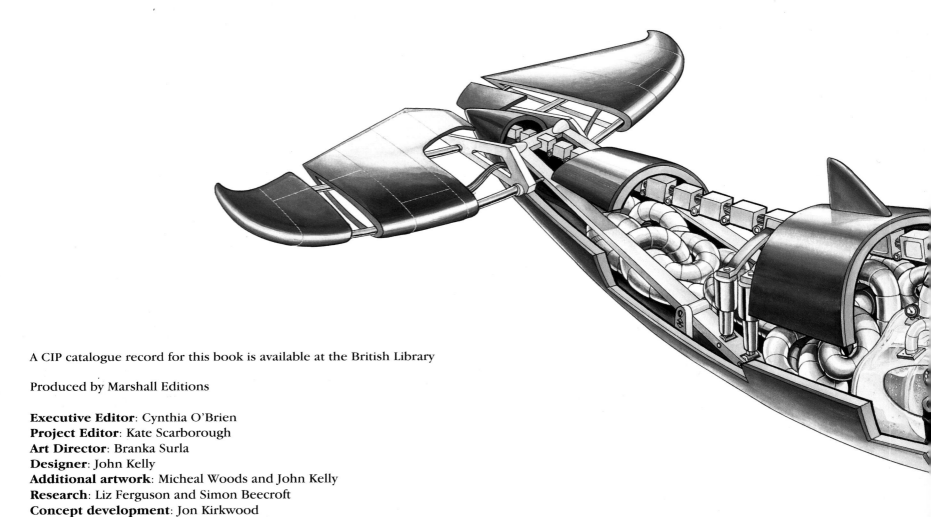

A CIP catalogue record for this book is available at the British Library

Produced by Marshall Editions

Executive Editor: Cynthia O'Brien
Project Editor: Kate Scarborough
Art Director: Branka Surla
Designer: John Kelly
Additional artwork: Micheal Woods and John Kelly
Research: Liz Ferguson and Simon Beecroft
Concept development: Jon Kirkwood

Editorial Director: Ruth Binney
Production: Barry Baker and Janice Storr

Originated by CLG, Verona, Italy
Printed and bound in Italy by Officine Grafiche De Agostini—Novara

The Robot Zoo

John Kelly
Dr Philip Whitfield and Obin

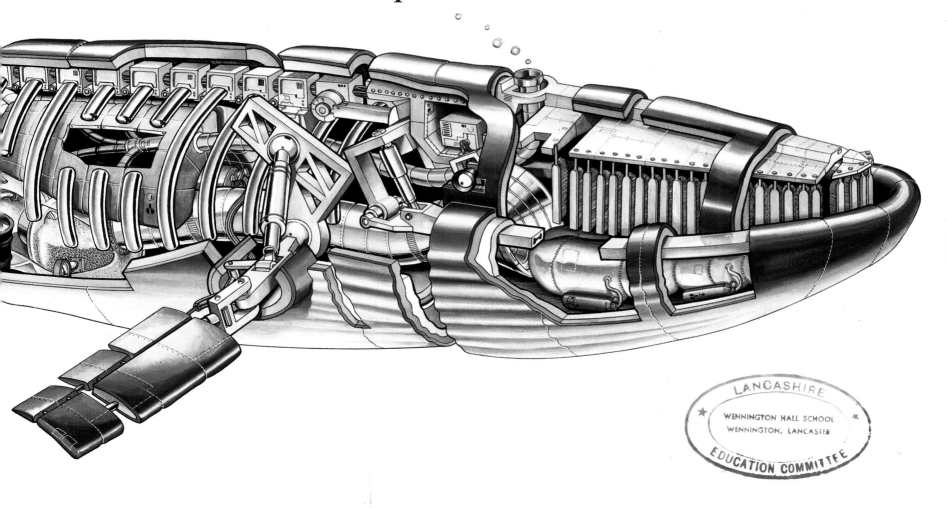

HAMLYN

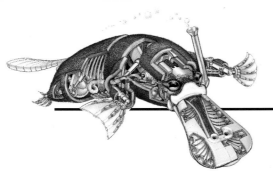

Contents

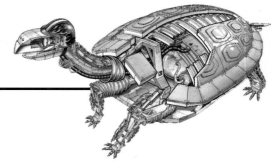

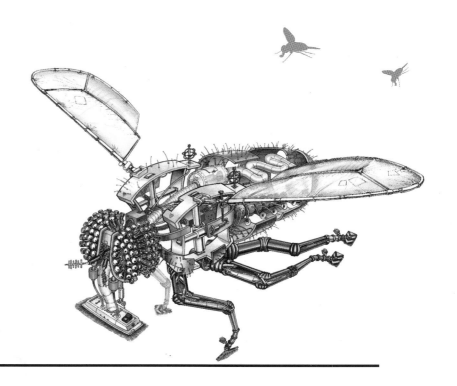

Introduction

Have you ever wondered how a gull's wings work or how a giant squid propels itself through the water, how a spider can spin a web or how a grasshopper sings? These are just some of the amazing things that the animals in this book can do. Nature is a master engineer and has designed every animal to be specially suited to its surroundings. You'd have thought that each animal was a carefully planned machine, because they are all so specifically adapted to their individual lifestyles.

Here in *The Robot Zoo*, we have made animals into machines. They are all copies of nature's own designs. Looking at them will help you to understand how real animals work, because inside they're all separated into parts that you might recognize. We've used shock absorbers for the giraffe's horns, strong armour for the rhino's thick skin and huge digging tools for the mole's front claws. We've even included a glossary at the back to help you every step of the way.

All animals move around, breathe, eat and avoid being eaten, and every creature manages to survive successfully in its own special way. Discover all sorts of inside secrets and find out for yourself how animals really work.

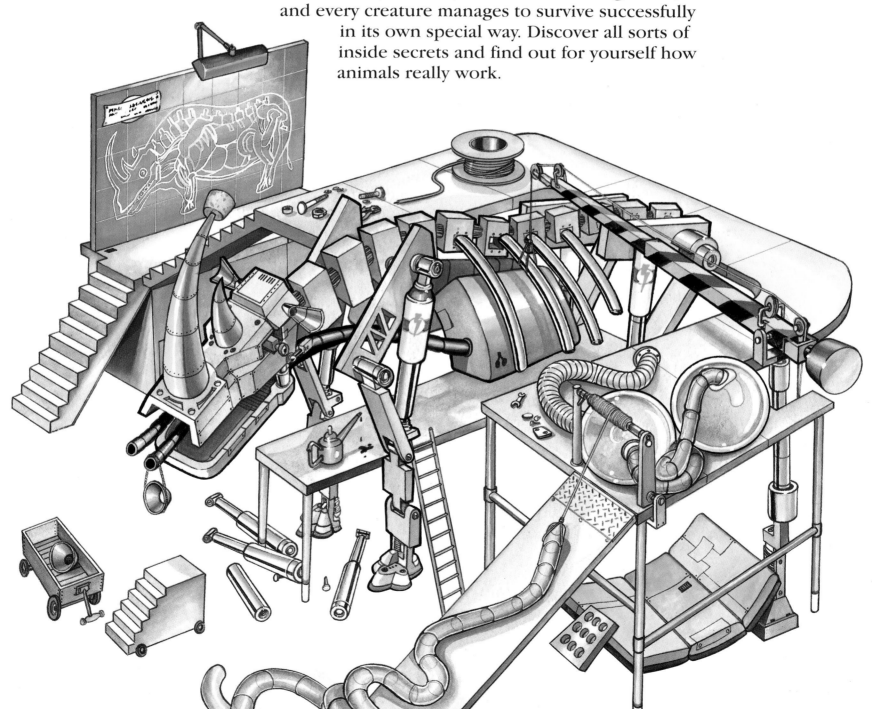

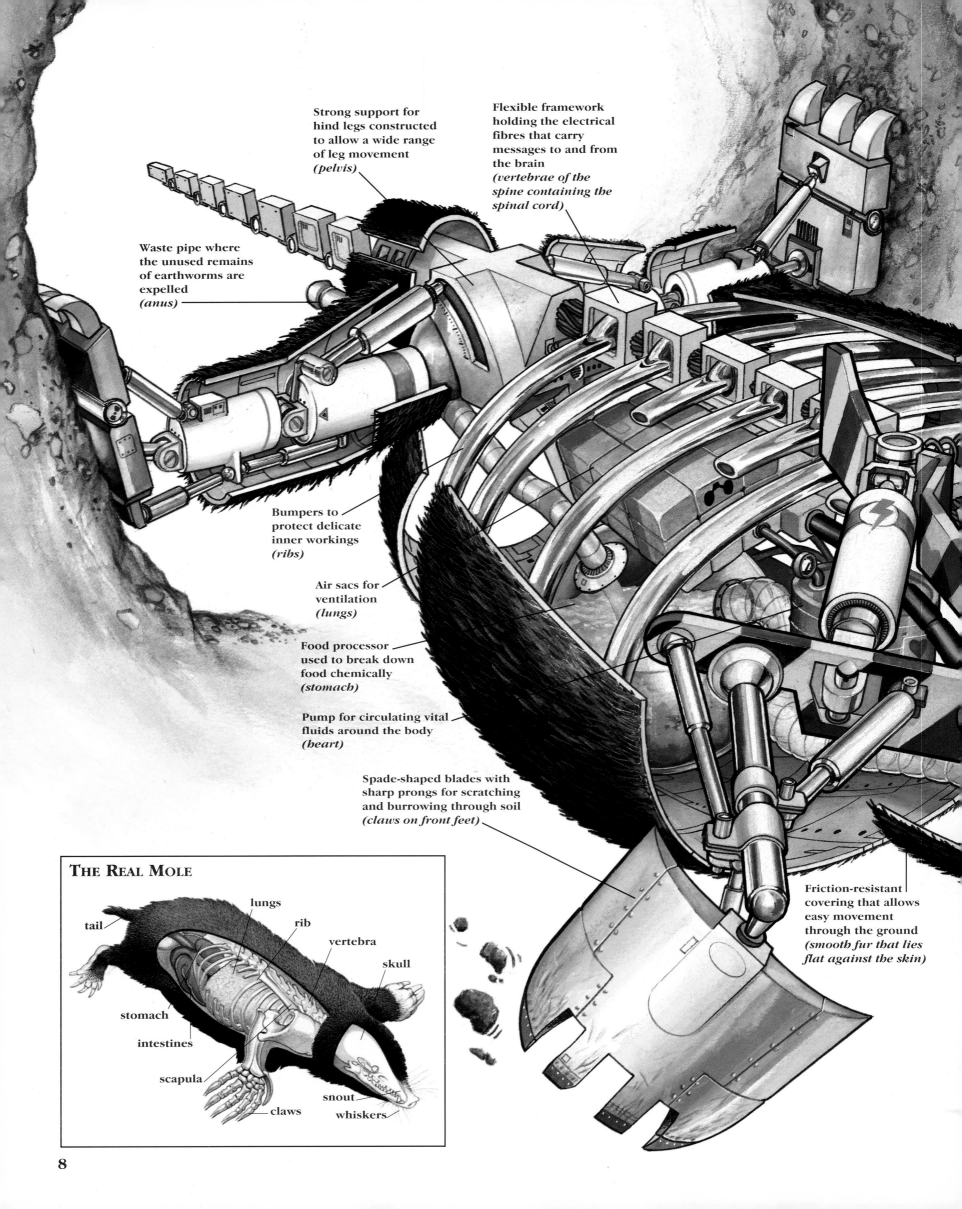

Strong support for hind legs constructed to allow a wide range of leg movement
(pelvis)

Flexible framework holding the electrical fibres that carry messages to and from the brain
(vertebrae of the spine containing the spinal cord)

Waste pipe where the unused remains of earthworms are expelled
(anus)

Bumpers to protect delicate inner workings
(ribs)

Air sacs for ventilation
(lungs)

Food processor used to break down food chemically
(stomach)

Pump for circulating vital fluids around the body
(heart)

Spade-shaped blades with sharp prongs for scratching and burrowing through soil
(claws on front feet)

Friction-resistant covering that allows easy movement through the ground
(smooth fur that lies flat against the skin)

THE REAL MOLE

tail

lungs

rib

vertebra

skull

stomach

intestines

scapula

snout

whiskers

claws

Mole

9

To enable the front arms to dig properly in the soil, the robot must brace itself against the sides of the tunnel. This prevents the robot from being pushed backwards as the front blades move forward. You can see that the hind legs are attached with swivel joints, which means they can be rotated sideways and pushed against the sides of the tunnel. The robot mole can then burrow efficiently.

Moles are mammals – they are warm-blooded animals that give birth to live young. The mole is related to insect-eating animals like shrews and hedgehogs. Moles are adapted for a life underground burrowing in the soil. It is no surprise that the machines we use for digging railway or mining tunnels are sometimes called mechanical moles – they do exactly the same job that the living mole does.

This cutaway robot mole shows how the animal can make a burrow in hard ground, push its way along the tunnel it has excavated and find food in the dark underground world in which it lives. The robot has special machinery, such as the extra-sensitive smell detectors for searching out earthworms and the shovel-like front claws for digging, to carry out each of these tasks.

Since the mole lives underground in the dark, vision is not very useful. Although it has no outer ear, which could be damaged during burrowing, its hearing is good. However, the mole relies most on its senses of smell and touch, which are especially developed in its nose and whiskers.

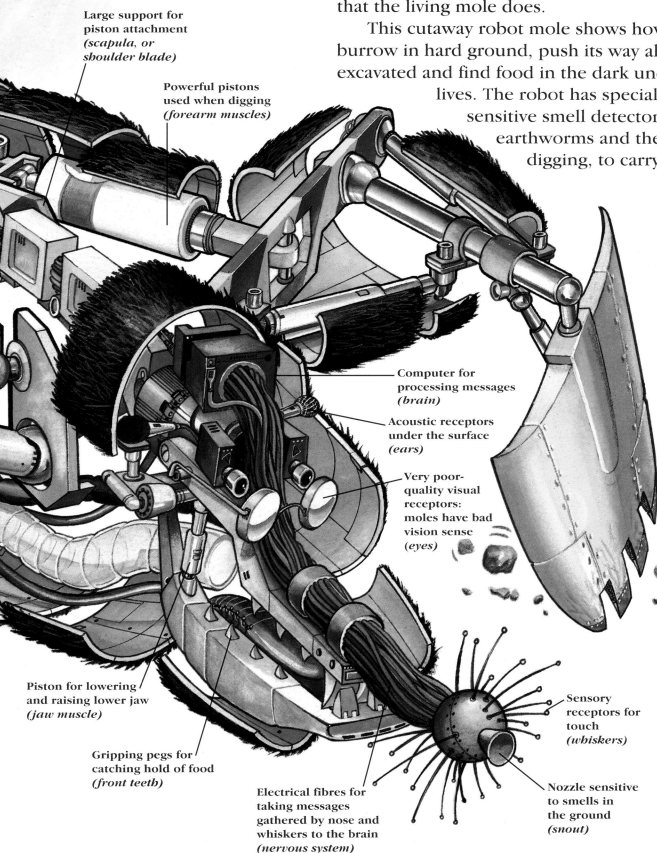

Large support for piston attachment (*scapula, or shoulder blade*)

Powerful pistons used when digging (*forearm muscles*)

Computer for processing messages (*brain*)

Acoustic receptors under the surface (*ears*)

Very poor-quality visual receptors: moles have bad vision sense (*eyes*)

Piston for lowering and raising lower jaw (*jaw muscle*)

Gripping pegs for catching hold of food (*front teeth*)

Electrical fibres for taking messages gathered by nose and whiskers to the brain (*nervous system*)

Sensory receptors for touch (*whiskers*)

Nozzle sensitive to smells in the ground (*snout*)

MOLE FACTS
Country: worldwide
Habitat: temperate climates, underground
Length: up to 23 cm (9 in)
Weight: up to 85 g (3 oz)
Closest relative: shrew

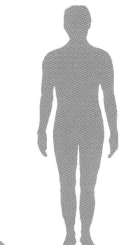

Spider

Even though some spiders are less than two millimetres across, you can see from this robot spider that they are highly complicated machines. Spiders are often mistakenly thought of as insects. In fact, they are arachnids, a completely different group of jointed-limbed arthropods that have eight legs. There are over thirty thousand different kinds of spiders. Some of the larger spiders can live for up to twenty-five years.

All spiders are predators. This means they have to find their food, trap it and kill it. Spiders eat insects, which are not the easiest animals to hunt – as you would know if you've ever tried to catch a fly. So almost all spiders produce silk threads which they form into a web. This helps them catch insects that fly past. But have you ever wondered how the spider makes its silk threads? And why insects get caught in them? Or how the spider kills its prey?

This robot version of a typical spider shows the types of machinery a spider needs to build webs, feed and make baby spiders.

How do spiders know how to make a web, what food they can eat and where to catch it? Their brains are like pre-programmed computers. They know instinctively how to behave. In any given situation, the spider's brain tells it what to do.

Spiders inject their prey with poison to kill it, and with substances called digestive enzymes that break down the insect's insides into a kind of soup. Once this has happened, the spider sucks up the liquid that has been made.

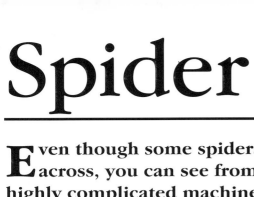

Sensory receptors used to locate vibrations of either prey or danger *(sensitive hairs)*

Pre-programmed mini-computer *(brain)*

Syringes to inject poison *(chelicerae, or fangs)*

Suction nozzle for intake of food that has been dissolved *(mouth)*

Jointed probes with sensors *(feelers called pedipalps that hold prey down and that can sense surroundings)*

Eight visual receptors on turrets, pointing in different directions *(eyes)*

Hollow tubes that can be moved by hydraulics *(legs moved with muscles)*

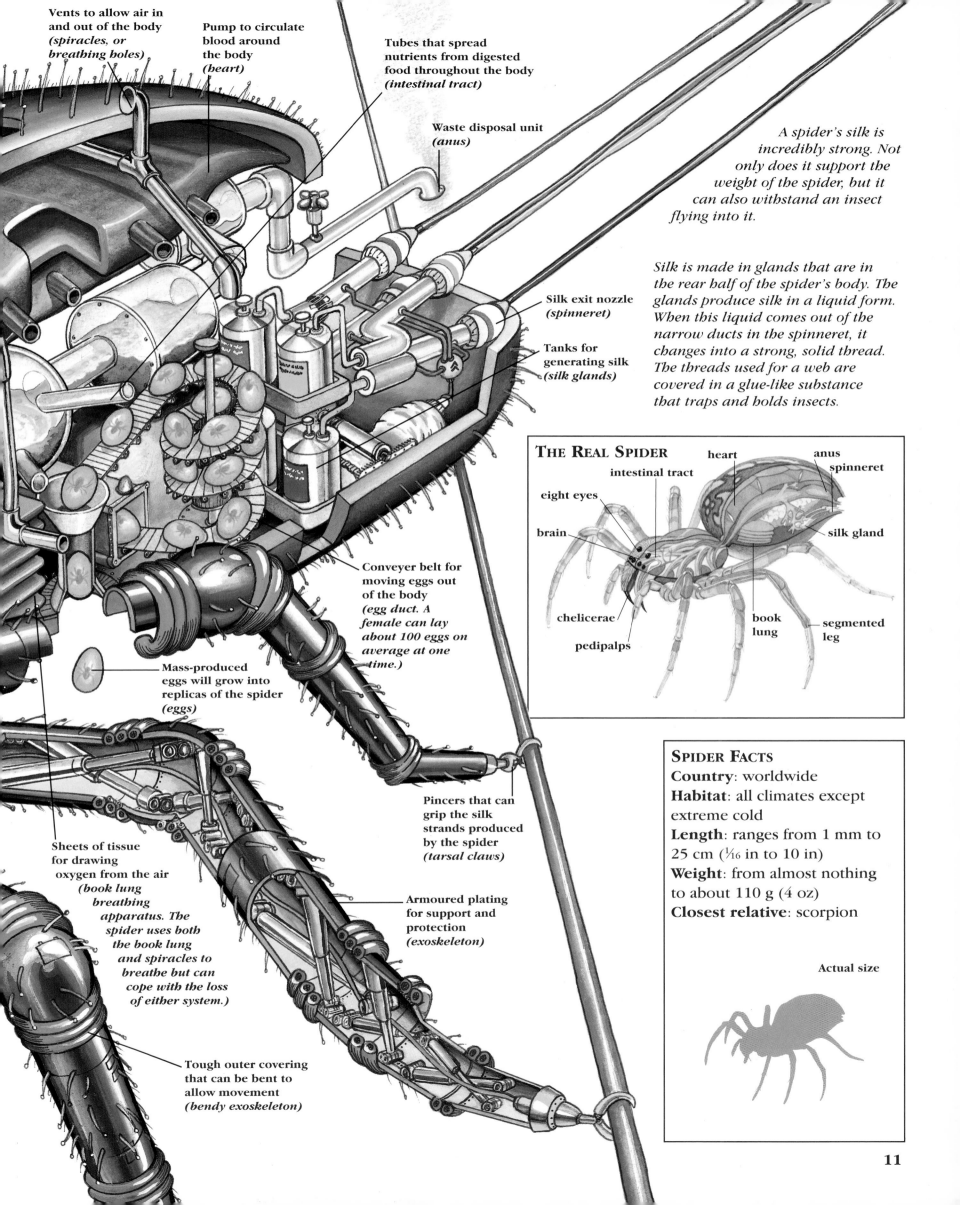

Vents to allow air in and out of the body (spiracles, or breathing holes)

Pump to circulate blood around the body (heart)

Tubes that spread nutrients from digested food throughout the body (intestinal tract)

Waste disposal unit (anus)

Silk exit nozzle (spinneret)

Tanks for generating silk (silk glands)

A spider's silk is incredibly strong. Not only does it support the weight of the spider, but it can also withstand an insect flying into it.

Silk is made in glands that are in the rear half of the spider's body. The glands produce silk in a liquid form. When this liquid comes out of the narrow ducts in the spinneret, it changes into a strong, solid thread. The threads used for a web are covered in a glue-like substance that traps and holds insects.

Conveyer belt for moving eggs out of the body (egg duct. A female can lay about 100 eggs on average at one time.)

Mass-produced eggs will grow into replicas of the spider (eggs)

Sheets of tissue for drawing oxygen from the air (book lung breathing apparatus. The spider uses both the book lung and spiracles to breathe but can cope with the loss of either system.)

Pincers that can grip the silk strands produced by the spider (tarsal claws)

Armoured plating for support and protection (exoskeleton)

Tough outer covering that can be bent to allow movement (bendy exoskeleton)

THE REAL SPIDER

heart

anus

spinneret

intestinal tract

eight eyes

brain

silk gland

chelicerae

book lung

segmented leg

pedipalps

SPIDER FACTS
Country: worldwide
Habitat: all climates except extreme cold
Length: ranges from 1 mm to 25 cm (1/16 in to 10 in)
Weight: from almost nothing to about 110 g (4 oz)
Closest relative: scorpion

Actual size

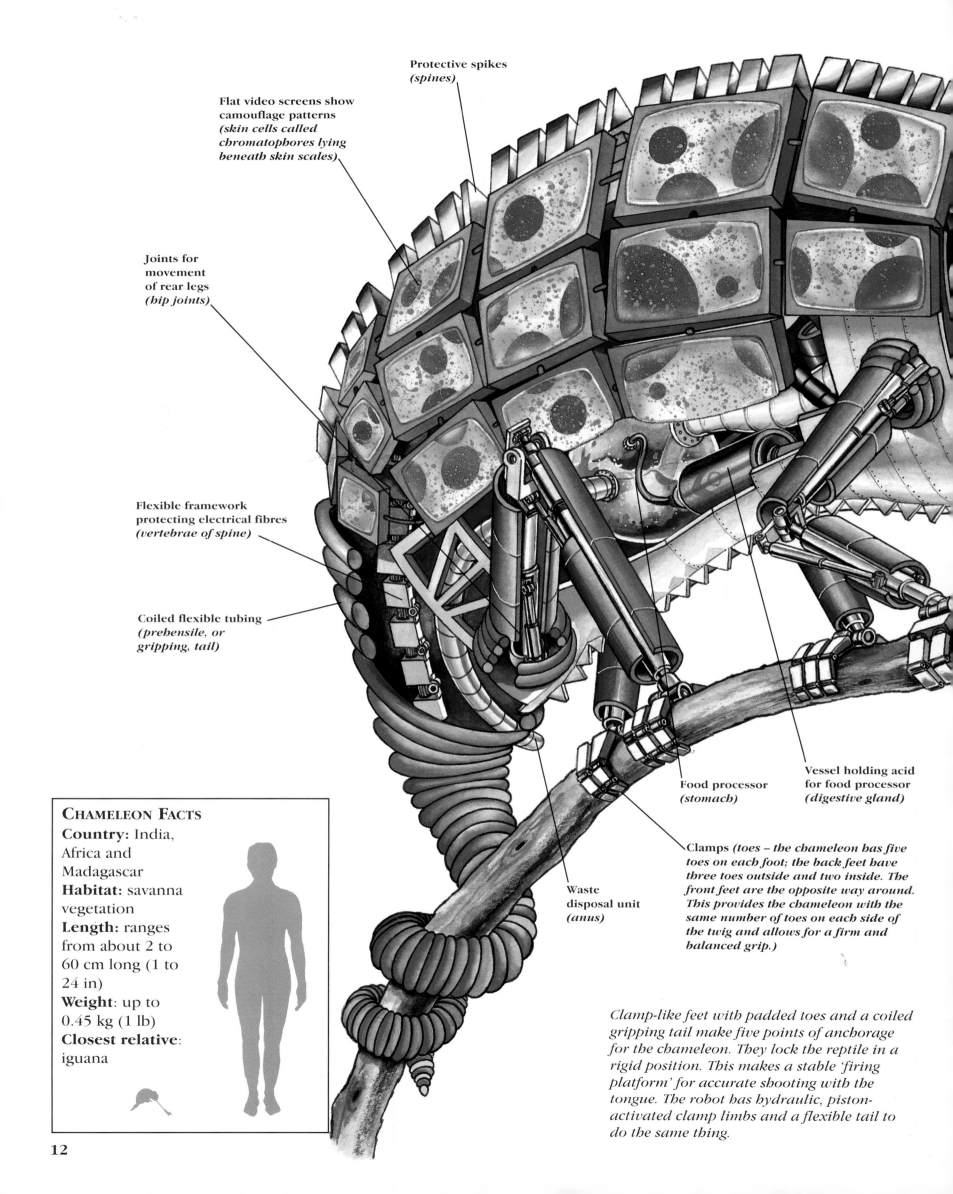

Protective spikes
(spines)

Flat video screens show
camouflage patterns
(skin cells called
chromatophores lying
beneath skin scales)

Joints for
movement
of rear legs
(hip joints)

Flexible framework
protecting electrical fibres
(vertebrae of spine)

Coiled flexible tubing
(prehensile, or
gripping, tail)

Food processor
(stomach)

Vessel holding acid
for food processor
(digestive gland)

Clamps (toes – the chameleon has five
toes on each foot; the back feet have
three toes outside and two inside. The
front feet are the opposite way around.
This provides the chameleon with the
same number of toes on each side of
the twig and allows for a firm and
balanced grip.)

Waste
disposal unit
(anus)

CHAMELEON FACTS
Country: India,
Africa and
Madagascar
Habitat: savanna
vegetation
Length: ranges
from about 2 to
60 cm long (1 to
24 in)
Weight: up to
0.45 kg (1 lb)
Closest relative:
iguana

*Clamp-like feet with padded toes and a coiled
gripping tail make five points of anchorage
for the chameleon. They lock the reptile in a
rigid position. This makes a stable 'firing
platform' for accurate shooting with the
tongue. The robot has hydraulic, piston-
activated clamp limbs and a flexible tail to
do the same thing.*

Chameleon

Mini-computer
(brain)

Electrical
control fibres
(nerve system)

Universal joints for
visual receptors
*(eye muscles which
allow the eyes to
move in all
directions)*

Protective
sleeves for visual
receptors
(eyelids)

Visual
receptors
(eyes)

Air and
scent inlets
(nostrils)

Spike around
which the spring
coil is wound
(bone)

Coil
(extendible tongue)

Spring-loaded
mechanism
*(muscles forcing
out the tongue)*

Air intake pipe
(trachea, or windpipe)

Food intake pipe
(oesophagus)

A chameleon is a reptile with two famous skills. First, it can change its skin colour and pattern to match its surroundings – from mottled brown on a tree trunk to bright green on a leafy twig. Second, it catches insects in a unique way. After walking very slowly up to an insect that it has located using its large, separately moveable eyes, the chameleon shoots out an immensely long, sticky-tipped tongue to trap its prey. Based on the design of a real rainforest chameleon, this robot can perform both of the reptile's party tricks.

The chameleon is the same as other reptiles, in that it is cold-blooded and it lays eggs. It is also part of a group of reptiles called lizards. Lizards feed at night and are very good climbers. Because of its ability to change colour, the chameleon is one of the most talented lizards.

The robot's two pivoting visual receptors pick up an excellent picture of the world around it. Control fibres from the receptors link back to the mini-computer. This computer, via other fibres, controls the images on the banks of tiny video screens that cover the robot's surface. With multi-screen picture software, the computer makes the robot's surface look like its surroundings. In the real animal, the eyes, brain and the nerves that run to colour cells in the skin do the same thing.

Flypaper
(sticky tongue end)

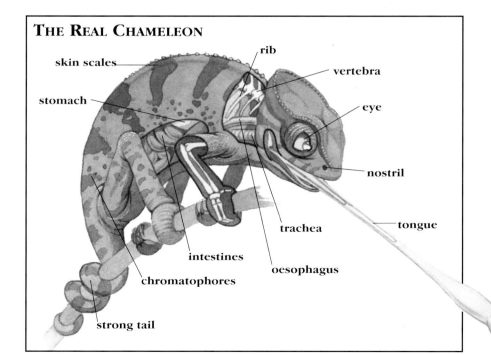

THE REAL CHAMELEON

skin scales

stomach

rib

vertebra

eye

nostril

trachea

tongue

intestines

oesophagus

chromatophores

strong tail

The chameleon's tongue is built out of a muscular tube wrapped around a long, thin tapering bone that lies in the floor of the animal's mouth. When the chameleon wants to catch its prey, its tongue muscles squeeze tightly on the bone. This makes the whole tongue shoot out like an orange pip squeezed between your fingers. In the robot, a spring-loaded mechanism triggers the food-capturing machinery, which is a long spring that uncoils and shoots forward. Good aim is achieved because the spring is coiled around a forward-pointing spike. The spring has a sticky end that allows the chameleon to capture a robot fly.

Platypus

When the first specimens of the platypus were brought to Europe from Australia two hundred years ago, scientists thought that they were fakes. They could not believe that the same animal could have fur, a beak like a duck, a tail like a beaver and the ability to lay eggs. Yet the platypus is real – it is a very rare egg-laying mammal.

Despite its strange appearance, the platypus is a superbly designed underwater hunter. It catches crayfish and worms on the bottom of muddy rivers where it is impossible to see. It is able to search for its food in darkness using its specially adapted beak-like snout. This is filled with sensors that can detect any movement in the murky water.

This mechanical platypus shows how the body parts of the animal work for swimming, capturing food, burrowing and laying eggs.

The beak-like snout is a device for finding prey in dark, muddy waters. Some of its sense endings can find food by touch. Others can pick up tiny electrical currents in the water that are given off by the nerves and muscles of the prey. The robot version has both pressure-pad sensors and tiny electrical sensors that do the same jobs.

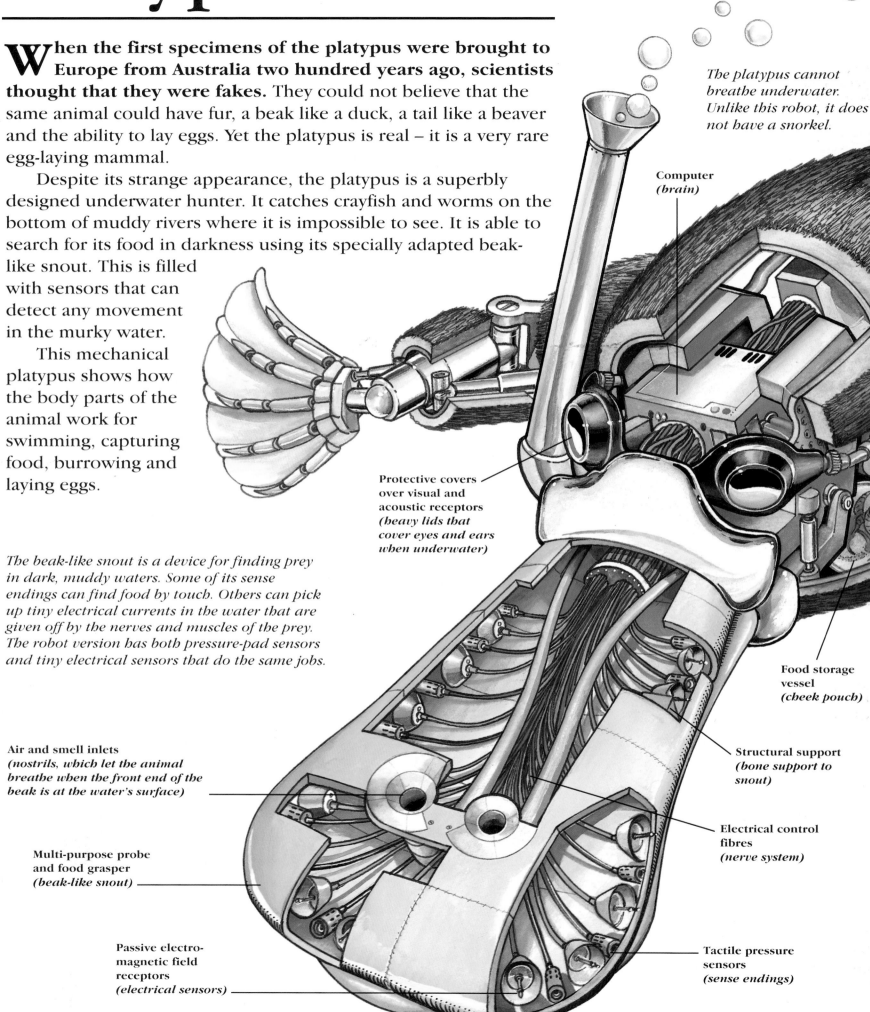

The platypus cannot breathe underwater. Unlike this robot, it does not have a snorkel.

Computer
(brain)

Protective covers over visual and acoustic receptors
(heavy lids that cover eyes and ears when underwater)

Food storage vessel
(cheek pouch)

Structural support
(bone support to snout)

Electrical control fibres
(nerve system)

Air and smell inlets
(nostrils, which let the animal breathe when the front end of the beak is at the water's surface)

Multi-purpose probe and food grasper
(beak-like snout)

Passive electro-magnetic field receptors
(electrical sensors)

Tactile pressure sensors
(sense endings)

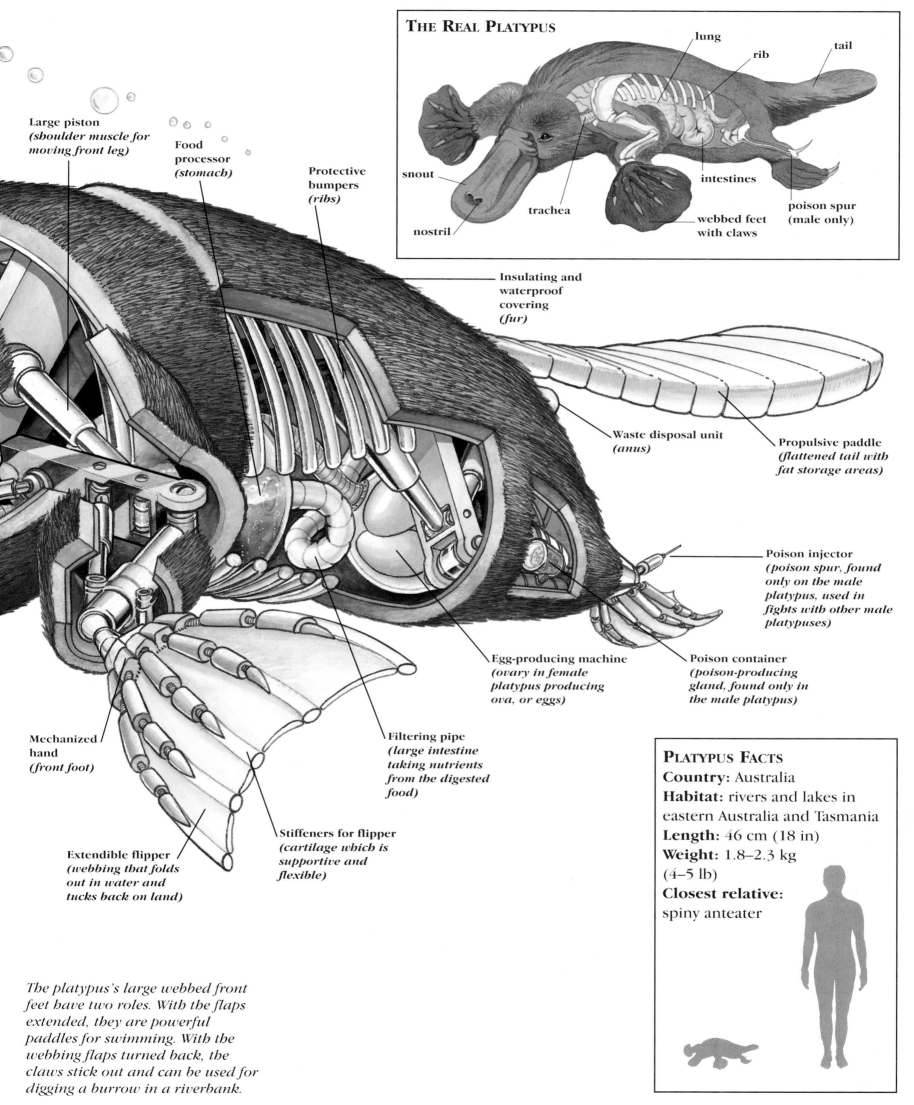

Large piston
*(shoulder muscle for
moving front leg)*

Food processor
(stomach)

Protective
bumpers
(ribs)

THE REAL PLATYPUS

lung

rib

tail

snout

intestines

nostril

trachea

poison spur
(male only)

webbed feet
with claws

Insulating and
waterproof
covering
(fur)

Waste disposal unit
(anus)

Propulsive paddle
*(flattened tail with
fat storage areas)*

Poison injector
*(poison spur, found
only on the male
platypus, used in
fights with other male
platypuses)*

Egg-producing machine
*(ovary in female
platypus producing
ova, or eggs)*

Poison container
*(poison-producing
gland, found only in
the male platypus)*

Mechanized
hand
(front foot)

Filtering pipe
*(large intestine
taking nutrients
from the digested
food)*

Stiffeners for flipper
*(cartilage which is
supportive and
flexible)*

Extendible flipper
*(webbing that folds
out in water and
tucks back on land)*

PLATYPUS FACTS
Country: Australia
Habitat: rivers and lakes in
eastern Australia and Tasmania
Length: 46 cm (18 in)
Weight: 1.8–2.3 kg
(4–5 lb)
Closest relative:
spiny anteater

*The platypus's large webbed front
feet have two roles. With the flaps
extended, they are powerful
paddles for swimming. With the
webbing flaps turned back, the
claws stick out and can be used for
digging a burrow in a riverbank.*

Bat

While birds rule the daytime skies, the bat, a flying mammal, is master of the air at night. Its leathery wings are very strong and efficient for flying. They are made of flexible skin flaps that stretch between the incredibly long fingers of the bat's hands. During the day, most bats usually roost in large groups in caves, attics or hollow trees, hanging upside-down by their clawed hind feet.

Most bats go hunting at night for food such as moths, but some have different ways of feeding. Vampire bats from South and Central America feed on the blood of people, cows and horses. Fruit bats, sometimes called flying foxes, feed on the fruit of tropical trees. Hunting bats catch mice on the ground or fish that swim near the surface of a lake.

Bats have a clever way of finding their food in complete darkness. They detect their prey using a system called echolocation. The bat sends out very high-pitched noises (ultrasonic sounds) that 'echo' or bounce off its prey. Using the echoes to locate its prey, the bat then chases, captures and eats it.

The 'fingers' that make up the robot's wings are lightweight tubes. The material between the tubes acts like a sail on a hang-glider, stretching back on to the hind legs and between the hind legs and tail. Pistons attached to the robot's body move the tubes of the wings up and down in flight.

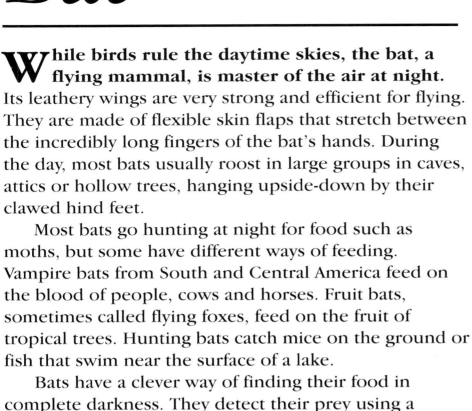

Strut
(second finger)

Strut
(third finger)

Strut
(fifth finger)

Strut
(fourth finger)

Strong, flexible material stretched over struts
(wing membrane)

Long support strut
(tail)

Filtering pipe *(intestines taking nutrients from the digested food)*

Extra strut for added membrane support *(bone called a calcar)*

Forward-facing clamps for gripping branches *(claws)*

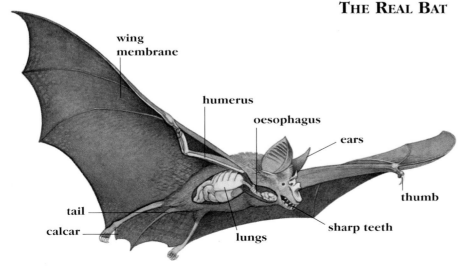

THE REAL BAT

wing membrane

humerus

oesophagus

ears

thumb

tail

calcar

lungs

sharp teeth

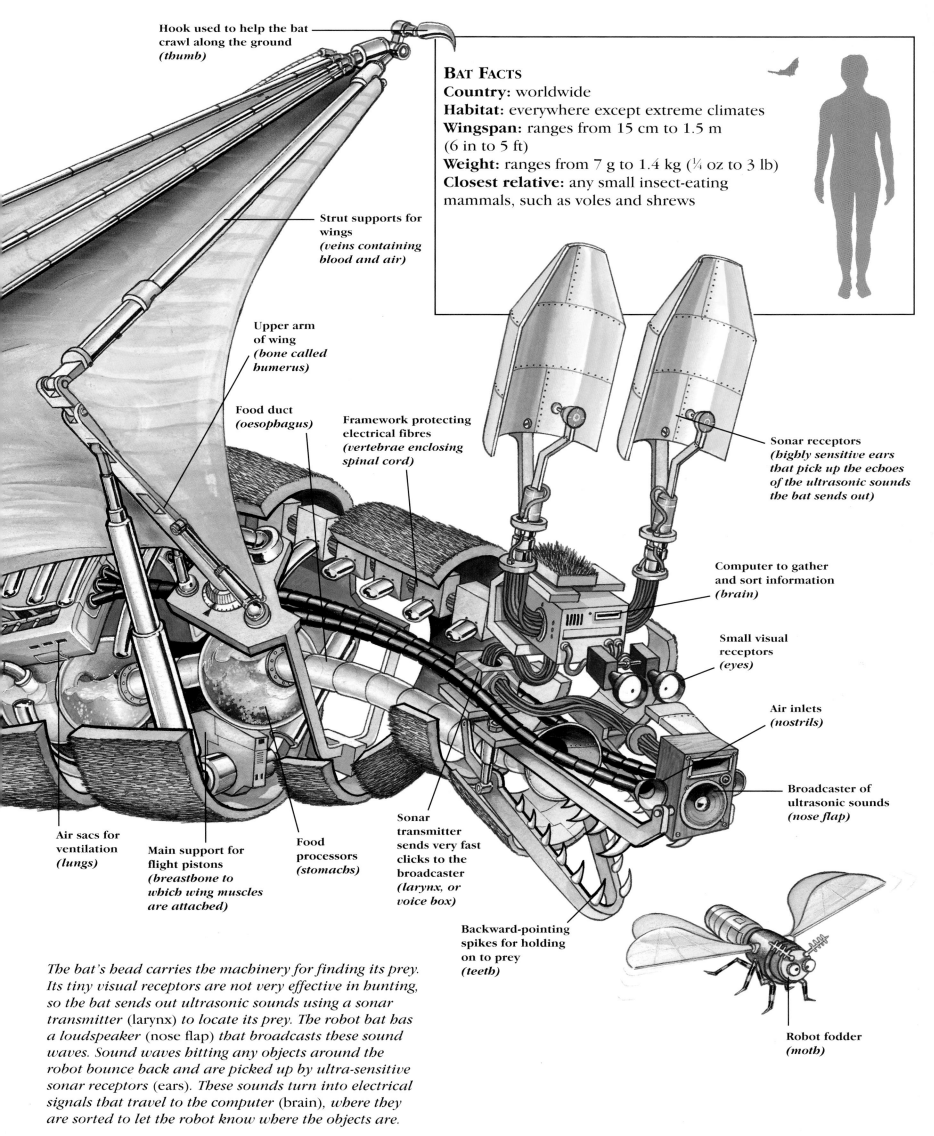

Hook used to help the bat crawl along the ground *(thumb)*

BAT FACTS
Country: worldwide
Habitat: everywhere except extreme climates
Wingspan: ranges from 15 cm to 1.5 m (6 in to 5 ft)
Weight: ranges from 7 g to 1.4 kg (¼ oz to 3 lb)
Closest relative: any small insect-eating mammals, such as voles and shrews

Strut supports for wings *(veins containing blood and air)*

Upper arm of wing *(bone called humerus)*

Food duct *(oesophagus)*

Framework protecting electrical fibres *(vertebrae enclosing spinal cord)*

Sonar receptors *(highly sensitive ears that pick up the echoes of the ultrasonic sounds the bat sends out)*

Computer to gather and sort information *(brain)*

Small visual receptors *(eyes)*

Air inlets *(nostrils)*

Broadcaster of ultrasonic sounds *(nose flap)*

Air sacs for ventilation *(lungs)*

Main support for flight pistons *(breastbone to which wing muscles are attached)*

Food processors *(stomachs)*

Sonar transmitter sends very fast clicks to the broadcaster *(larynx, or voice box)*

Backward-pointing spikes for holding on to prey *(teeth)*

Robot fodder *(moth)*

The bat's head carries the machinery for finding its prey. Its tiny visual receptors are not very effective in hunting, so the bat sends out ultrasonic sounds using a sonar transmitter (larynx) *to locate its prey. The robot bat has a loudspeaker* (nose flap) *that broadcasts these sound waves. Sound waves hitting any objects around the robot bounce back and are picked up by ultra-sensitive sonar receptors* (ears). *These sounds turn into electrical signals that travel to the computer* (brain), *where they are sorted to let the robot know where the objects are.*

Giraffe

Giraffes are the tallest animals on Earth.

Giraffes are the tallest animals on Earth. This is an advantage in the wild, but it can create a lot of problems too. So, to cope with their amazing height, giraffes have special solutions. This giraffe, made of strong mechanical parts, shows just how unusual the natural systems of this animal have to be for the body to move and work successfully.

First of all, the giraffe needs an incredibly strong heart to pump blood up its long neck and to its brain. When the giraffe bends down, the surge of blood down to the head could cause problems with pressure, so the arteries at the base of its neck slow the flow of the blood until the animal brings its neck up again. Look at the robot giraffe's neck to see the many pressure valves that regulate the blood as it is pumped up the long neck tube.

You might wonder why the giraffe doesn't fall over, since the front part of its body is so much bigger than the back. In fact, most of the giraffe's weight is at the back. The weight of the neck and head is carried over its long front legs and is supported by powerful muscles that are attached to its shoulders and backbone. This allows the giraffe to stand tall and eat leaves that are far beyond the reach of other animals.

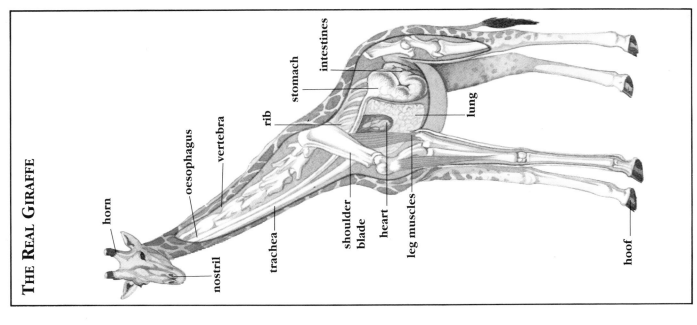

THE REAL GIRAFFE

- intestines
- stomach
- lung
- rib
- vertebra
- oesophagus
- heart
- leg muscles
- shoulder blade
- trachea
- horn
- nostril
- hoof

Moveable acoustic receptors for following sounds (*ears*)

Shock absorbers (*horns*)

Visual receptors (*eyes*)

Long, flexible pad for grabbing food and water (*tongue*)

Files for grinding up tough plants (*back teeth*)

Sharp blades for snipping leaves (*front teeth*)

Air intake pipe (*trachea, or windpipe*)

Air inlets (*nostrils*)

Food is squeezed down through a flexible tube (*oesophagus*)

High-pressure flexible tubing (*artery*)

Flexible framework fits together to support the neck (*neck vertebrae*)

Valves stop the blood from falling back down the neck between the beats of the pump (*valves in arteries*)

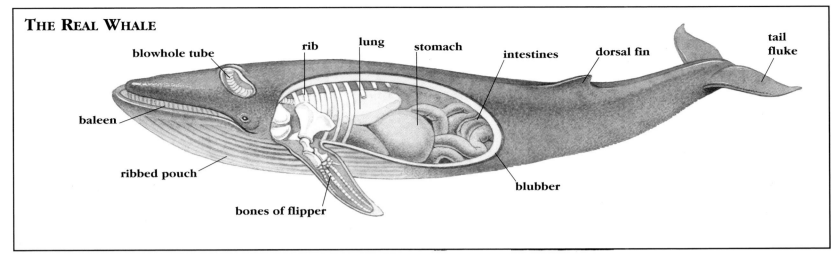

THE REAL WHALE

blowhole tube

rib

lung

stomach

intestines

dorsal fin

tail fluke

baleen

ribbed pouch

bones of flipper

blubber

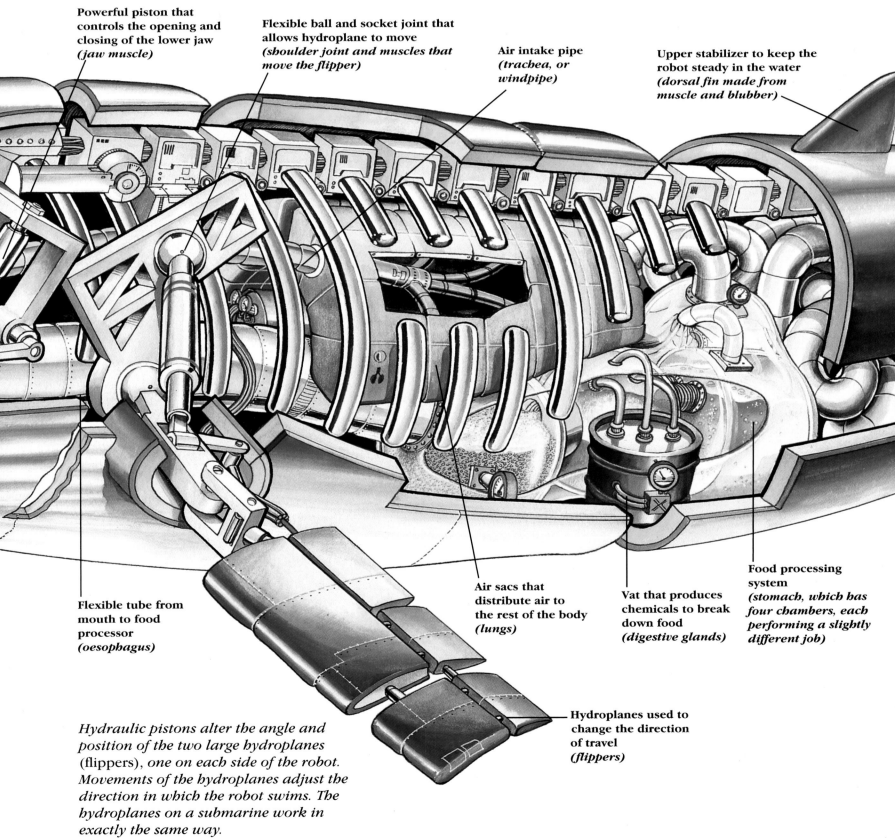

Powerful piston that controls the opening and closing of the lower jaw *(jaw muscle)*

Flexible ball and socket joint that allows hydroplane to move *(shoulder joint and muscles that move the flipper)*

Air intake pipe *(trachea, or windpipe)*

Upper stabilizer to keep the robot steady in the water *(dorsal fin made from muscle and blubber)*

Flexible tube from mouth to food processor *(oesophagus)*

Air sacs that distribute air to the rest of the body *(lungs)*

Vat that produces chemicals to break down food *(digestive glands)*

Food processing system *(stomach, which has four chambers, each performing a slightly different job)*

Hydroplanes used to change the direction of travel *(flippers)*

Hydraulic pistons alter the angle and position of the two large hydroplanes (flippers), one on each side of the robot. Movements of the hydroplanes adjust the direction in which the robot swims. The hydroplanes on a submarine work in exactly the same way.

22

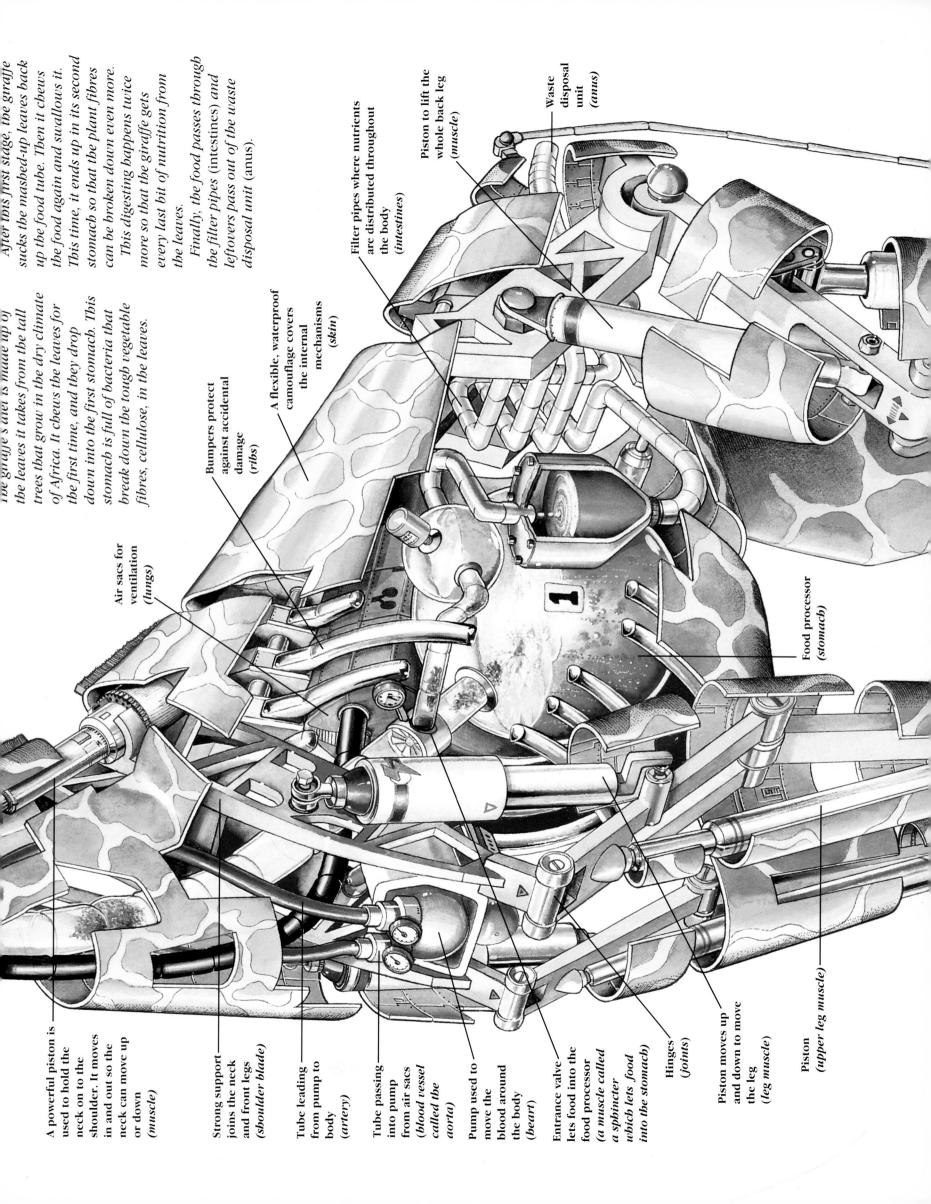

The giraffe's diet is made up of the leaves it takes from the tall trees that grow in the dry climate of Africa. It chews the leaves for the first time, and they drop down into the first stomach. This stomach is full of bacteria that break down the tough vegetable fibres, cellulose, in the leaves.

After this first stage, the giraffe sucks the mashed-up leaves back up the food tube. Then it chews the food again and swallows it. This time, it ends up in its second stomach so that the plant fibres can be broken down even more.

This digesting happens twice and more so that the giraffe gets every last bit of nutrition from the leaves.

Finally, the food passes through the filter pipes (intestines) and leftovers pass out of the waste disposal unit (anus).

Filter pipes where nutrients are distributed throughout the body (intestines)

Piston to lift the whole back leg (muscle)

Waste disposal unit (anus)

A flexible, waterproof camouflage covers the internal mechanisms (skin)

Bumpers protect against accidental damage (ribs)

Food processor (stomach)

Air sacs for ventilation (lungs)

A powerful piston is used to hold the neck on to the shoulder. It moves in and out so the neck can move up or down (muscle)

Strong support joins the neck and front legs (shoulder blade)

Tube leading from pump to body (artery)

Tube passing into pump from air sacs (blood vessel called the aorta)

Pump used to move the blood around the body (heart)

Entrance valve lets food into the food processor (a muscle called a sphincter which lets food into the stomach)

Hinges (joints)

Piston moves up and down to move the leg (leg muscle)

Piston (upper leg muscle)

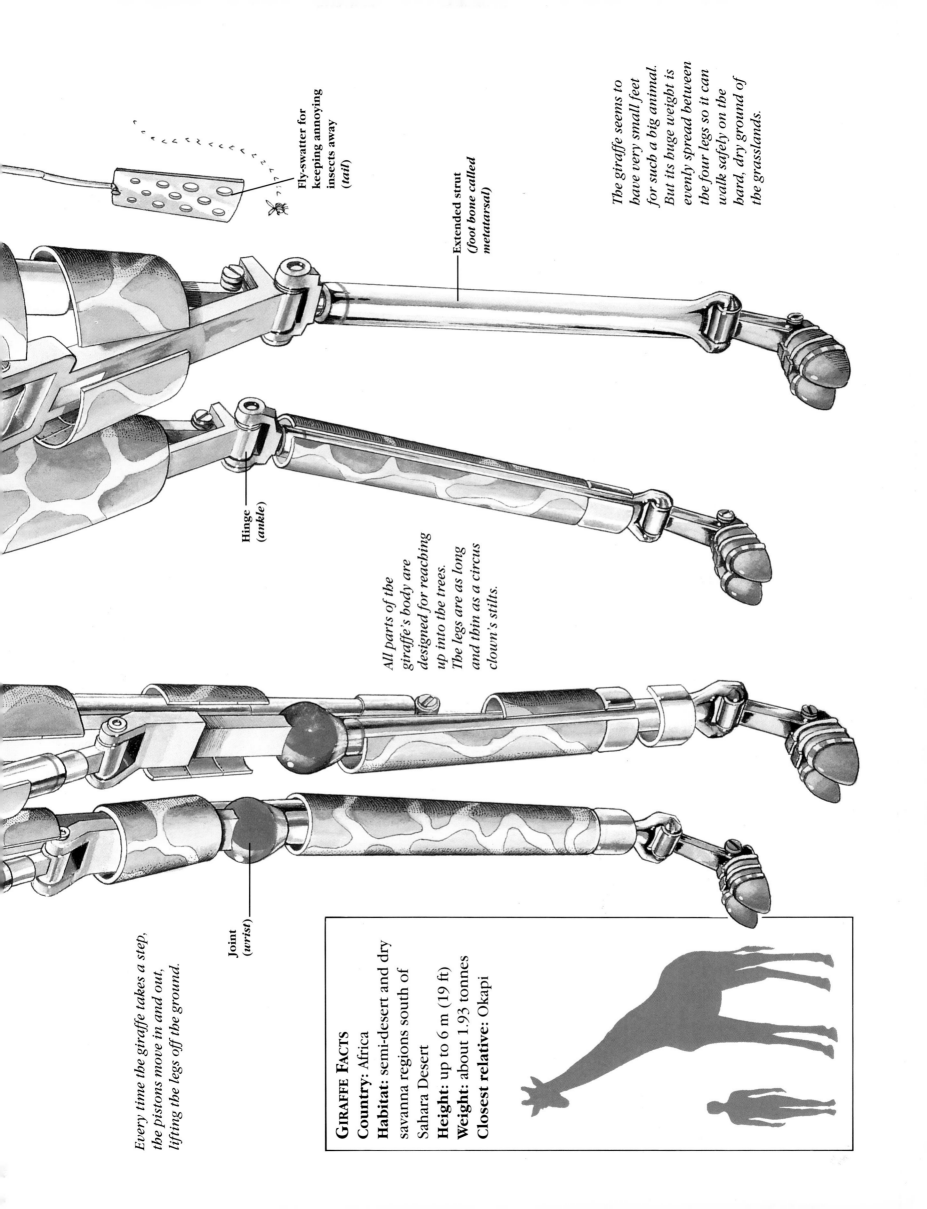

Fly-swatter for keeping annoying insects away *(tail)*

Extended strut *(foot bone called metatarsal)*

The giraffe seems to have very small feet for such a big animal. But its huge weight is evenly spread between the four legs so it can walk safely on the hard, dry ground of the grasslands.

Hinge *(ankle)*

All parts of the giraffe's body are designed for reaching up into the trees. The legs are as long and thin as a circus clown's stilts.

Joint *(wrist)*

Every time the giraffe takes a step, the pistons move in and out, lifting the legs off the ground.

GIRAFFE FACTS
Country: Africa
Habitat: semi-desert and dry savanna regions south of Sahara Desert
Height: up to 6 m (19 ft)
Weight: about 1.93 tonnes
Closest relative: Okapi

Blue Whale

The largest animal that has ever lived on this planet is the extraordinary blue whale. With a body shaped like a nuclear submarine, the whale is an air-breathing mammal that spends its whole life in the sea. Taking huge breaths in through the blowhole on the top of its head, it can dive deep into the ocean. It feeds underwater, gulping up countless thousands of shrimp-like animals called krill.

Although the blue whale is descended from land animals with four legs, its front legs have evolved into huge flippers that control the direction of its swimming, and its hind legs have disappeared altogether. The blue whale also has a vast and powerful tail to propel it through the water.

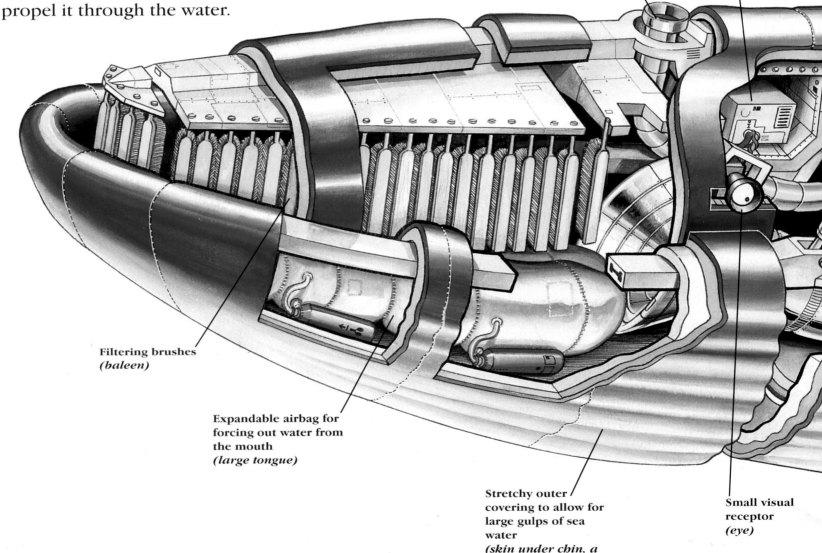

Large computer for processing information and controlling output *(brain)*

Air vent *(blowhole)*

Filtering brushes *(baleen)*

Expandable airbag for forcing out water from the mouth *(large tongue)*

Stretchy outer covering to allow for large gulps of sea water *(skin under chin, a ribbed pouch)*

Small visual receptor *(eye)*

The blue whale feeds by swimming through krill-rich seas. It opens its huge mouth, which fills with water and krill. Closing its mouth, it traps the krill inside filters called baleen (the curtain of brushes in the robot whale). The whale then uses its powerful tongue to force the water out through the baleen. When this happens, the krill are passed down to the oesophagus and swallowed.

The air vent (blowhole) *at the top of the head section is connected to the air storage sacs* (lungs) *that provide the robot with air while it is underwater. When the whale is submerged, the vent is covered to stop water from rushing into the air supply, which would be deadly.*

The outer casing of the robot is silky smooth and slips through the water with little resistance. Underneath this thin but strong and flexible casing is a thick layer of fatty insulating material (blubber). This prevents the inner working parts of the robot from cooling down too much in the cold ocean water.

The whale's tail is made from cartilage, not from bone. Cartilage is very strong and flexible, which makes it ideal as a propeller. The tail can measure up to 4.5 metres (15 feet) across and can push the whale through the water at speeds of up to 30 km/h (20 mph).

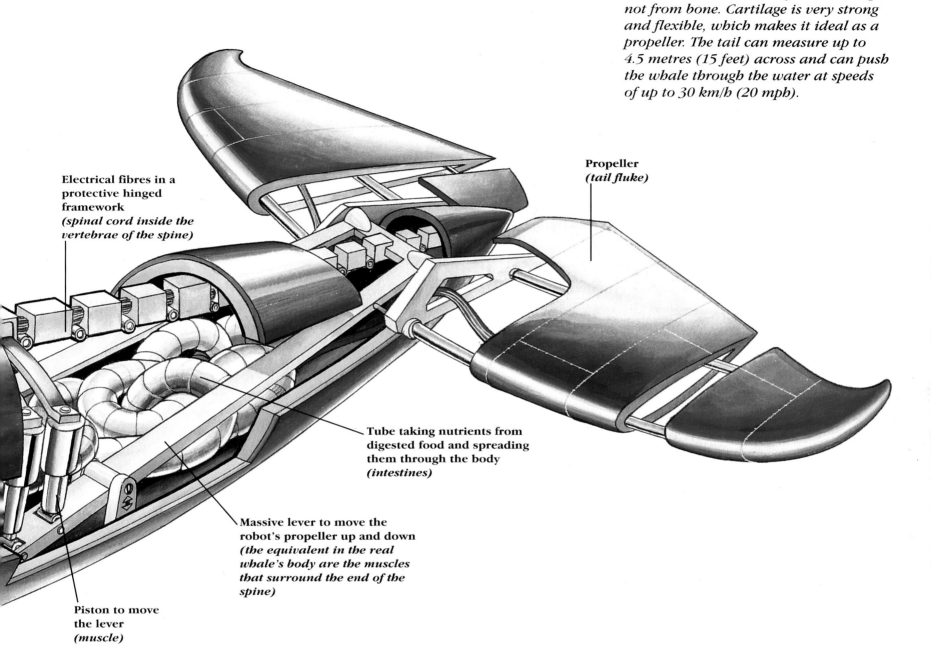

Electrical fibres in a protective hinged framework *(spinal cord inside the vertebrae of the spine)*

Propeller *(tail fluke)*

Tube taking nutrients from digested food and spreading them through the body *(intestines)*

Massive lever to move the robot's propeller up and down *(the equivalent in the real whale's body are the muscles that surround the end of the spine)*

Piston to move the lever *(muscle)*

BLUE WHALE FACTS
Habitat: deep seas and oceans worldwide
Length: up to 30 m (100 ft)
Weight: about 135 tonnes
Closest relative: other types of whale

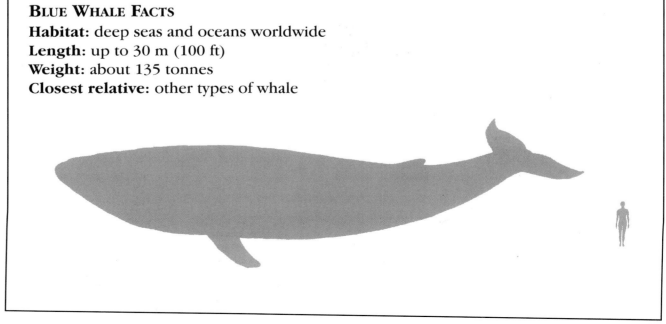

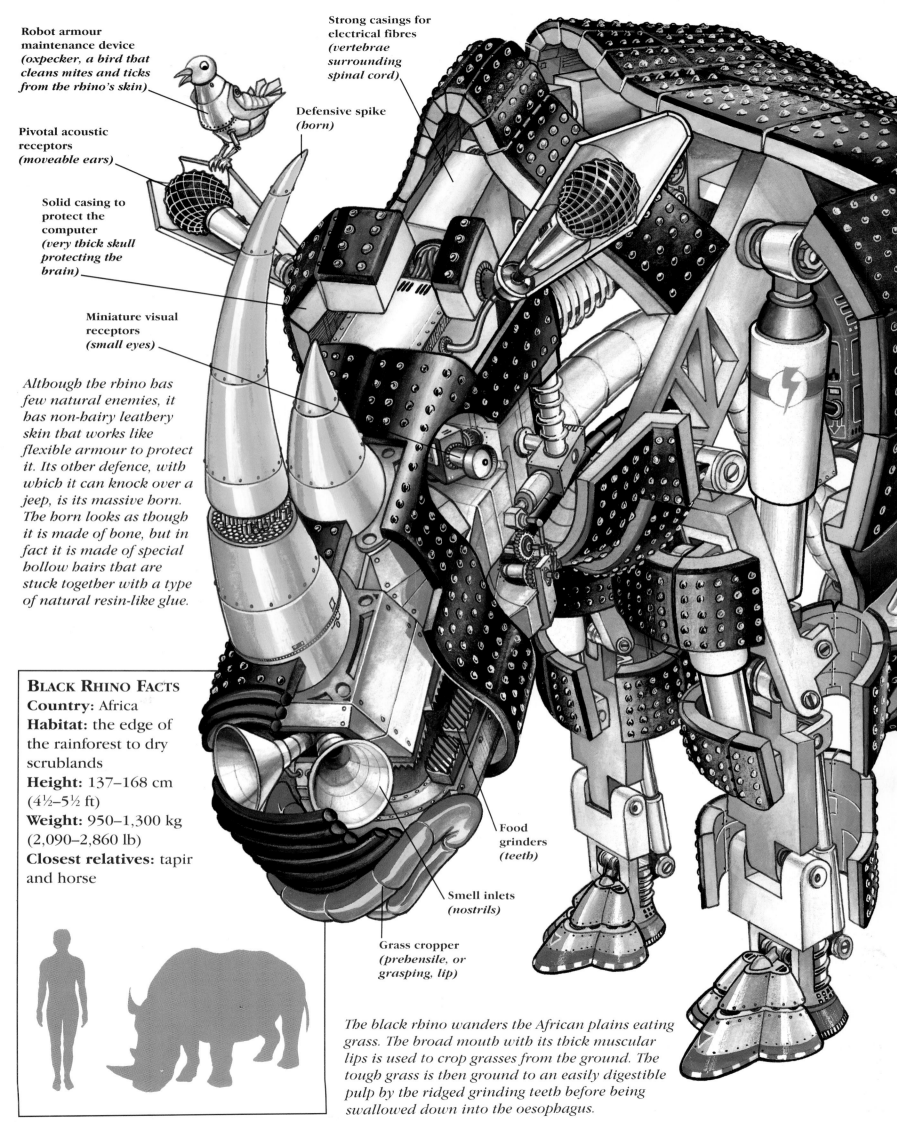

Robot armour maintenance device *(oxpecker, a bird that cleans mites and ticks from the rhino's skin)*

Pivotal acoustic receptors *(moveable ears)*

Solid casing to protect the computer *(very thick skull protecting the brain)*

Miniature visual receptors *(small eyes)*

Strong casings for electrical fibres *(vertebrae surrounding spinal cord)*

Defensive spike *(horn)*

Although the rhino has few natural enemies, it has non-hairy leathery skin that works like flexible armour to protect it. Its other defence, with which it can knock over a jeep, is its massive horn. The horn looks as though it is made of bone, but in fact it is made of special hollow hairs that are stuck together with a type of natural resin-like glue.

Food grinders *(teeth)*

Smell inlets *(nostrils)*

Grass cropper *(prehensile, or grasping, lip)*

Black Rhino Facts
Country: Africa
Habitat: the edge of the rainforest to dry scrublands
Height: 137–168 cm (4½–5½ ft)
Weight: 950–1,300 kg (2,090–2,860 lb)
Closest relatives: tapir and horse

The black rhino wanders the African plains eating grass. The broad mouth with its thick muscular lips is used to crop grasses from the ground. The tough grass is then ground to an easily digestible pulp by the ridged grinding teeth before being swallowed down into the oesophagus.

Rhinoceros

Dual food processors
(stomachs: the rhino is a ruminant like the giraffe)

Filtering pipe
(intestines)

After the elephant, the black rhino is one of the largest land mammals on Earth. It lives in and feeds on the grassland savannas of Africa. The rhino belongs to a group of animals with hoofs called ungulates. Its closest relatives are tapirs and horses, but only the rhino has ended up with a very heavy body carried on immensely strong legs.

The robot rhino is massive, just like the living animal. Its leg struts are incredibly sturdy, and each one has three weight-bearing props (toes) at the end. Instead of leathery skin, it has studded armour for extra protection. And it has a horn, which is made of incredibly strong sections that match the strength of the hollow, hair-like fibres in the real rhino's horn. The robot rhino even has a robot tick bird called an oxpecker to clean its armour.

Ball and socket joint
(hip joint anchored into rigid pelvis)

Flies and ticks that irritate the rhino can be brushed off with the hair-tipped tail or the large hair-fringed ears. Those out of reach of either of these fly-swatters are often removed by helpful tick birds such as oxpeckers. These companions perch on the rhino and eat the insects and ticks that live on it. This cleans the rhino's skin and protects the rhino from the diseases that can be carried by insects.

Fly-swatter
(tail)

Hinge joints with large pistons for movement
(the femur, tibia and fibula bones with muscles attached)

Three extra-strong supports
(toes ending in rounded hoofs)

Shock-absorbing pad
(flattened foot)

The rhino's legs end in flattened feet which together bear the animal's great weight. Each foot has three wide toes, each ending in a broad rounded hoof – the splayed-out toes and hoofs spread the rhino's weight over a large area.

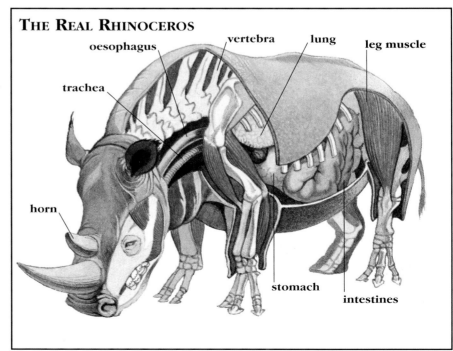

THE REAL RHINOCEROS

oesophagus

vertebra

lung

leg muscle

trachea

horn

stomach

intestines

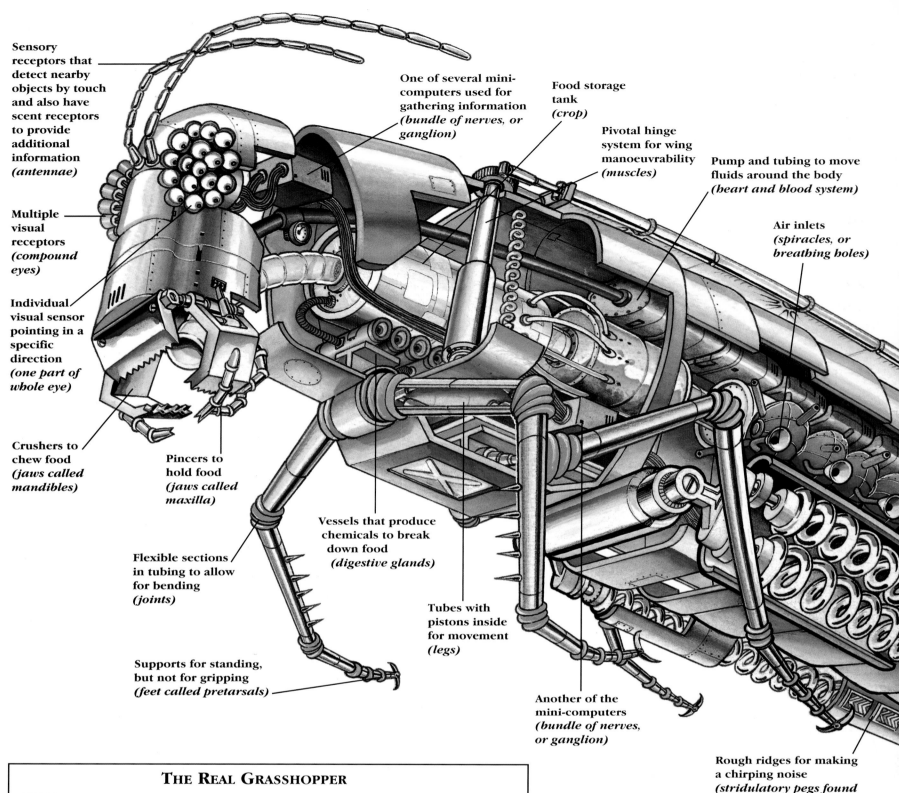

Sensory receptors that detect nearby objects by touch and also have scent receptors to provide additional information *(antennae)*

Multiple visual receptors *(compound eyes)*

Individual visual sensor pointing in a specific direction *(one part of whole eye)*

Crushers to chew food *(jaws called mandibles)*

Pincers to hold food *(jaws called maxilla)*

Flexible sections in tubing to allow for bending *(joints)*

Supports for standing, but not for gripping *(feet called pretarsals)*

One of several mini-computers used for gathering information *(bundle of nerves, or ganglion)*

Food storage tank *(crop)*

Pivotal hinge system for wing manoeuvrability *(muscles)*

Pump and tubing to move fluids around the body *(heart and blood system)*

Air inlets *(spiracles, or breathing holes)*

Vessels that produce chemicals to break down food *(digestive glands)*

Tubes with pistons inside for movement *(legs)*

Another of the mini-computers *(bundle of nerves, or ganglion)*

Rough ridges for making a chirping noise *(stridulatory pegs found on male grasshoppers)*

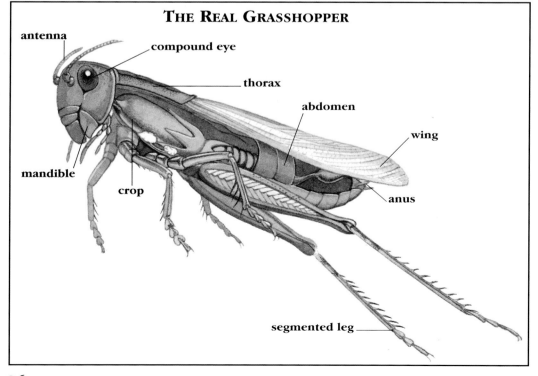

THE REAL GRASSHOPPER

antenna

compound eye

thorax

abdomen

wing

mandible

crop

anus

segmented leg

Inside the long rear section – the abdomen – is most of the intestine and the long heart. Insects such as the grasshopper do not have lungs. Instead, tubes connected to many openings called spiracles take air from the outside directly to the insect's tissues.

The grasshopper does not have a control centre or brain like other animals. Its nervous system is connected to various bundles of nerves around the body called ganglia.

Grasshopper

A grasshopper is an insect that lives in and feeds on grass and other plants. Using its huge hind legs, the grasshopper makes gigantic leaps into the air. Once airborne after its spring-assisted take-off, it can unfurl its two pairs of wings and continue flying with them.

Like all insects, the grasshopper has six legs. The two rear legs are specialized and strengthened for jumping, while the front two pairs are used only for walking on the ground. The grasshopper's head has two antennae that are able to feel and smell what is nearby. It also has two compound eyes that are made up of hundreds of tiny individual eyes. Each individual eye is called an ommatidium and has its own lens and light-sensitive cells, but they work together to provide an overall picture of a wide area surrounding the grasshopper. The mouthparts are a set of moveable jaws that let the grasshopper chomp its way through blades of grass.

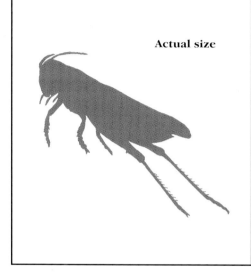

GRASSHOPPER FACTS
Country: worldwide
Habitat: found on the ground and on vegetation; the majority of grasshoppers live in meadows, fields and hedges
Length: up to 8 cm (3 in), but mostly 15–30 mm (0.6–1.2 in.)
Closest relatives: stick insect and cricket

Actual size

Flight enablers
(wings that can be unfurled for flight)

Waste disposal unit
(anus)

Hinge joints allow legs to bend
(knees)

Massive springs used to launch into the jump
(muscles)

Like all insects, the grasshopper has a body divided into three sections – the head, the thorax and the abdomen. The large abdomen is made of ten overlapping sections, each with a spiracle (a breathing hole) on both sides of the body. These sections can move against each other, which makes the abdomen flexible.

Look carefully at the back legs and you will see another special feature of the male grasshopper. There are file-like ridges (stridulatory pegs) on the inner side of the leg. They can be rubbed against the side of the robot's body to make a loud rasping noise to signal to other grasshopper robots. Living male grasshoppers make their chirping songs in the same way. They do this to attract females and to mark their territory.

The robot's main jumping legs are many-jointed and contain long and powerful springs. They can be compressed before a jump and then suddenly released to throw the robot into the air. Once in the air, the grasshopper uses its wings to fly.

27

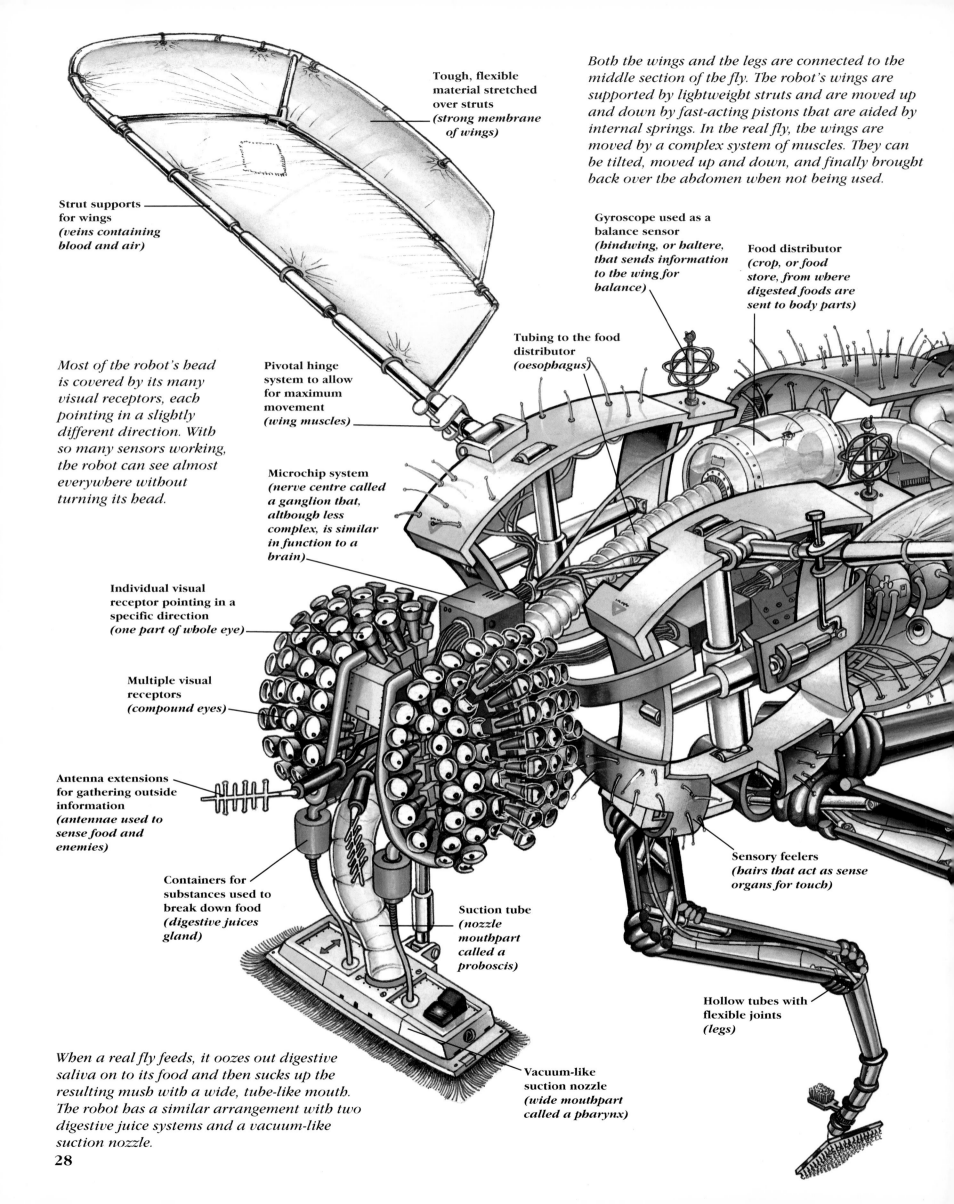

Tough, flexible material stretched over struts
(strong membrane of wings)

Both the wings and the legs are connected to the middle section of the fly. The robot's wings are supported by lightweight struts and are moved up and down by fast-acting pistons that are aided by internal springs. In the real fly, the wings are moved by a complex system of muscles. They can be tilted, moved up and down, and finally brought back over the abdomen when not being used.

Strut supports for wings
(veins containing blood and air)

Gyroscope used as a balance sensor
(hindwing, or haltere, that sends information to the wing for balance)

Food distributor
(crop, or food store, from where digested foods are sent to body parts)

Most of the robot's head is covered by its many visual receptors, each pointing in a slightly different direction. With so many sensors working, the robot can see almost everywhere without turning its head.

Pivotal hinge system to allow for maximum movement
(wing muscles)

Tubing to the food distributor
(oesophagus)

Microchip system
(nerve centre called a ganglion that, although less complex, is similar in function to a brain)

Individual visual receptor pointing in a specific direction
(one part of whole eye)

Multiple visual receptors
(compound eyes)

Antenna extensions for gathering outside information
(antennae used to sense food and enemies)

Sensory feelers
(hairs that act as sense organs for touch)

Containers for substances used to break down food
(digestive juices gland)

Suction tube
(nozzle mouthpart called a proboscis)

Hollow tubes with flexible joints
(legs)

When a real fly feeds, it oozes out digestive saliva on to its food and then sucks up the resulting mush with a wide, tube-like mouth. The robot has a similar arrangement with two digestive juice systems and a vacuum-like suction nozzle.

Vacuum-like suction nozzle
(wide mouthpart called a pharynx)

28

House Fly

Try to catch a fly and you will find out just how fast it can move. With huge compound eyes that are made up of hundreds of separate tiny eyes, the fly sees your hand coming. In a buzz of fast-beating wings, it is gone before you can touch it.

Although it is only the size of an adult's fingernail, the fly is an amazingly complicated animal. Its body is made up of three sections. The head contains the big eyes and mouth. The mid-section, or thorax, has three pairs of many-jointed legs plus two wings. A hind section, the abdomen, holds all the other body organs. Most of the body is covered in tiny hairs that let the fly detect pressure and vibrations. There is no skeleton inside a fly. Instead, the outer skin of the body, called the cuticle, is stiff and shell-like and makes a type of outer skeleton, or exoskeleton. This robot fly is built in a similar way with a rigid casing on each of its sections.

Waste disposal tubing *(intestines)*

Rigid outer casing for support and shape *(exoskeleton)*

Air inlets *(spiracles, or breathing holes)*

Sensory pads with hooked endings for extra grip *(clinging feet with taste organs on them)*

Cleaning brush used for grooming *(bristles on inside of legs)*

FLY FACTS
Country: worldwide
Habitat: in all places and climates except the very hot and the very cold
Length: 1 cm (½ in.)
Weight: almost nothing
Closest relatives: mosquitoes and horseflies

Actual size

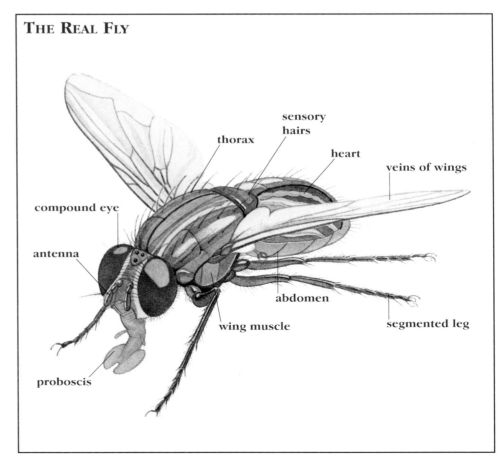

THE REAL FLY

sensory hairs

thorax

heart

veins of wings

compound eye

antenna

abdomen

segmented leg

wing muscle

proboscis

Giant Squid

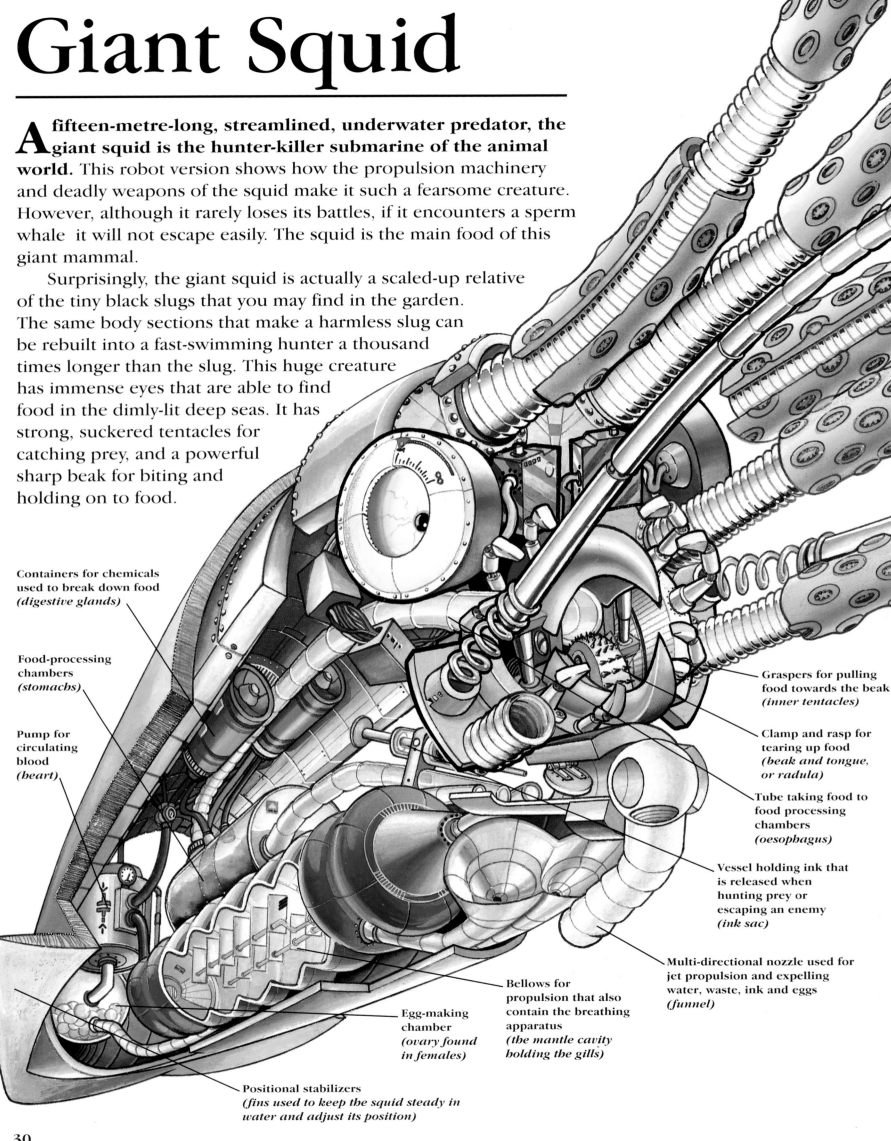

A fifteen-metre-long, streamlined, underwater predator, the giant squid is the hunter-killer submarine of the animal world. This robot version shows how the propulsion machinery and deadly weapons of the squid make it such a fearsome creature. However, although it rarely loses its battles, if it encounters a sperm whale it will not escape easily. The squid is the main food of this giant mammal.

Surprisingly, the giant squid is actually a scaled-up relative of the tiny black slugs that you may find in the garden. The same body sections that make a harmless slug can be rebuilt into a fast-swimming hunter a thousand times longer than the slug. This huge creature has immense eyes that are able to find food in the dimly-lit deep seas. It has strong, suckered tentacles for catching prey, and a powerful sharp beak for biting and holding on to food.

Containers for chemicals
used to break down food
(digestive glands)

Food-processing
chambers
(stomachs)

Pump for
circulating
blood
(heart)

Graspers for pulling
food towards the beak
(inner tentacles)

Clamp and rasp for
tearing up food
*(beak and tongue,
or radula)*

Tube taking food to
food processing
chambers
(oesophagus)

Vessel holding ink that
is released when
hunting prey or
escaping an enemy
(ink sac)

Multi-directional nozzle used for
jet propulsion and expelling
water, waste, ink and eggs
(funnel)

Bellows for
propulsion that also
contain the breathing
apparatus
*(the mantle cavity
holding the gills)*

Egg-making
chamber
*(ovary found
in females)*

Positional stabilizers
*(fins used to keep the squid steady in
water and adjust its position)*

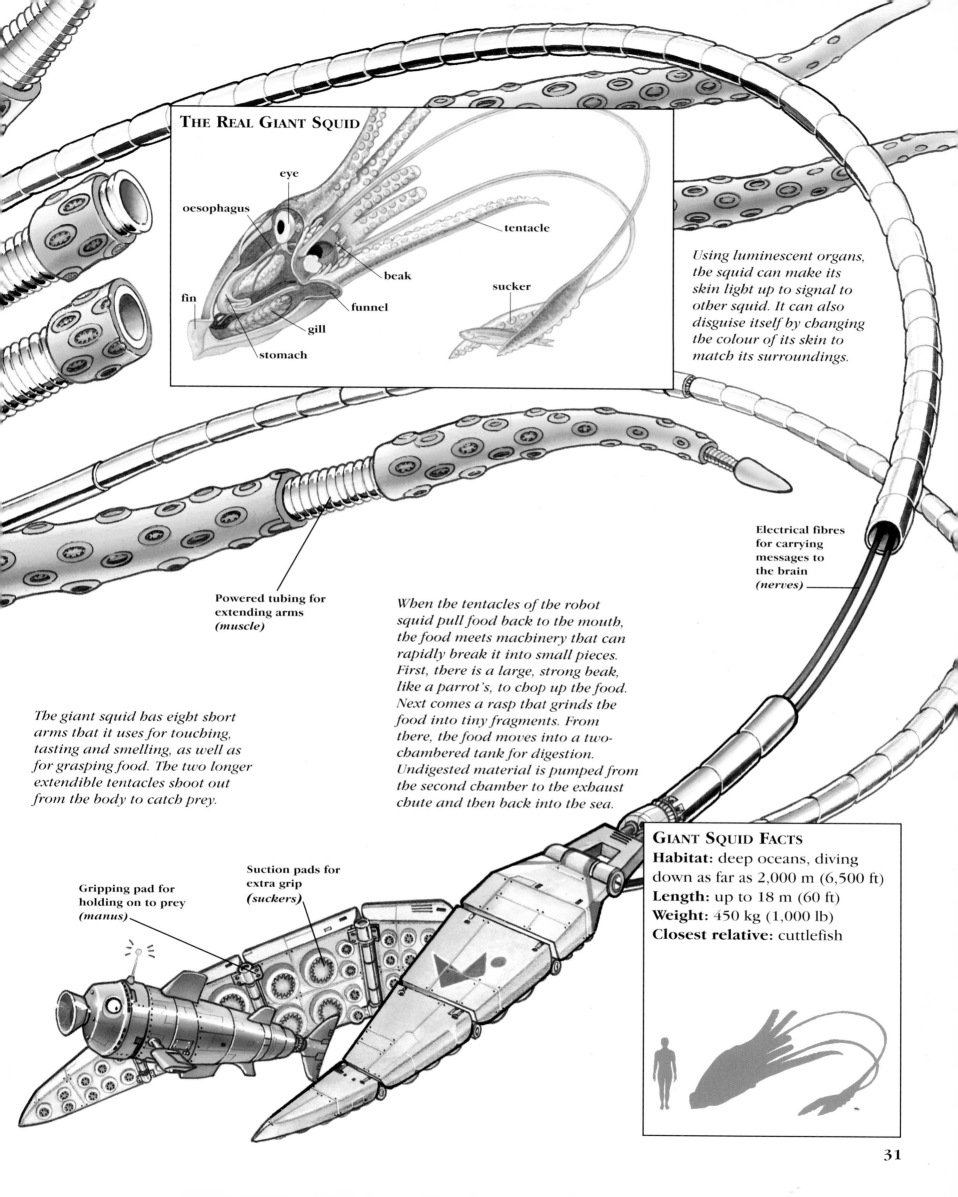

THE REAL GIANT SQUID

eye

oesophagus

tentacle

beak

fin

sucker

funnel

gill

stomach

Using luminescent organs, the squid can make its skin light up to signal to other squid. It can also disguise itself by changing the colour of its skin to match its surroundings.

Electrical fibres for carrying messages to the brain (nerves)

Powered tubing for extending arms (muscle)

When the tentacles of the robot squid pull food back to the mouth, the food meets machinery that can rapidly break it into small pieces. First, there is a large, strong beak, like a parrot's, to chop up the food. Next comes a rasp that grinds the food into tiny fragments. From there, the food moves into a two-chambered tank for digestion. Undigested material is pumped from the second chamber to the exhaust chute and then back into the sea.

The giant squid has eight short arms that it uses for touching, tasting and smelling, as well as for grasping food. The two longer extendible tentacles shoot out from the body to catch prey.

Gripping pad for holding on to prey (manus)

Suction pads for extra grip (suckers)

GIANT SQUID FACTS
Habitat: deep oceans, diving down as far as 2,000 m (6,500 ft)
Length: up to 18 m (60 ft)
Weight: 450 kg (1,000 lb)
Closest relative: cuttlefish

31

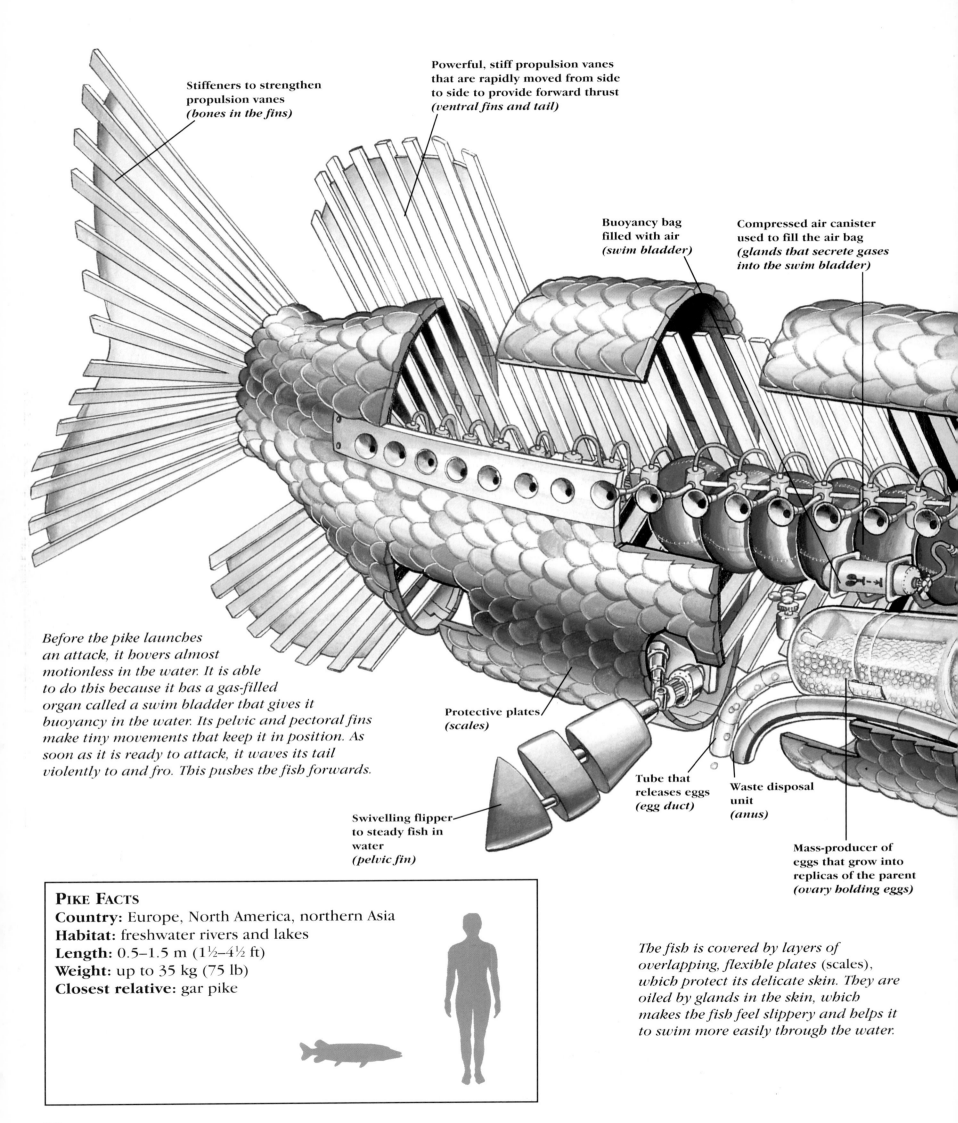

Stiffeners to strengthen
propulsion vanes
(bones in the fins)

Powerful, stiff propulsion vanes
that are rapidly moved from side
to side to provide forward thrust
(ventral fins and tail)

Buoyancy bag
filled with air
(swim bladder)

Compressed air canister
used to fill the air bag
*(glands that secrete gases
into the swim bladder)*

Protective plates
(scales)

Tube that
releases eggs
(egg duct)

Waste disposal
unit
(anus)

Swivelling flipper
to steady fish in
water
(pelvic fin)

Mass-producer of
eggs that grow into
replicas of the parent
(ovary holding eggs)

*Before the pike launches
an attack, it hovers almost
motionless in the water. It is able
to do this because it has a gas-filled
organ called a swim bladder that gives it
buoyancy in the water. Its pelvic and pectoral fins
make tiny movements that keep it in position. As
soon as it is ready to attack, it waves its tail
violently to and fro. This pushes the fish forwards.*

PIKE FACTS
Country: Europe, North America, northern Asia
Habitat: freshwater rivers and lakes
Length: 0.5–1.5 m (1½–4½ ft)
Weight: up to 35 kg (75 lb)
Closest relative: gar pike

*The fish is covered by layers of
overlapping, flexible plates (scales),
which protect its delicate skin. They are
oiled by glands in the skin, which
makes the fish feel slippery and helps it
to swim more easily through the water.*

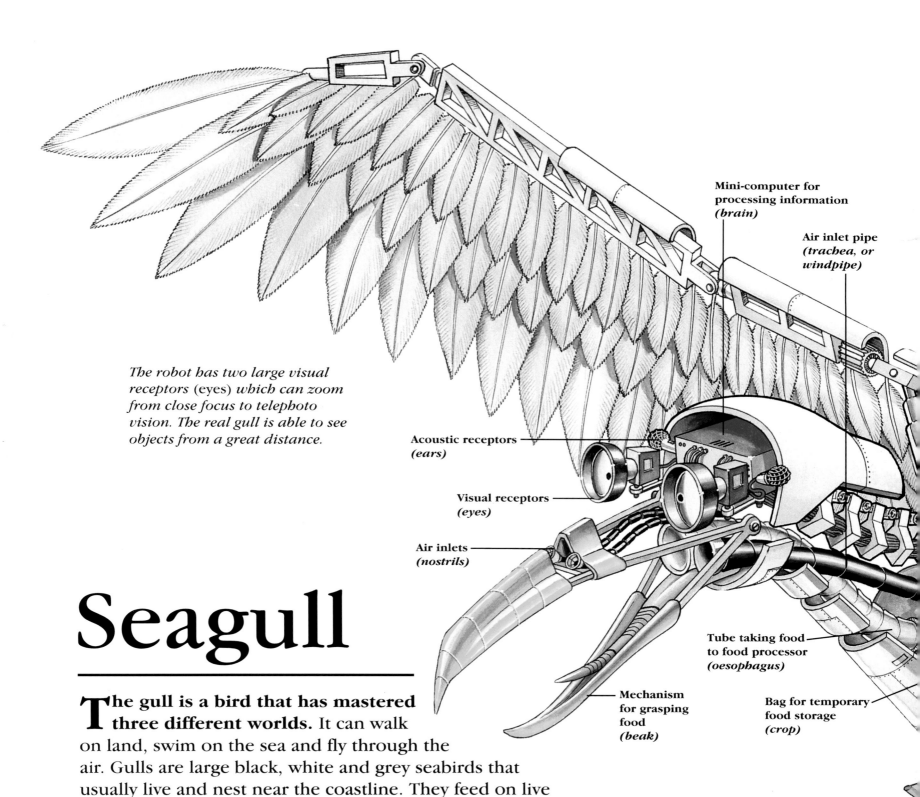

The robot has two large visual receptors (eyes) *which can zoom from close focus to telephoto vision. The real gull is able to see objects from a great distance.*

Mini-computer for processing information *(brain)*

Air inlet pipe *(trachea, or windpipe)*

Acoustic receptors *(ears)*

Visual receptors *(eyes)*

Air inlets *(nostrils)*

Tube taking food to food processor *(oesophagus)*

Mechanism for grasping food *(beak)*

Bag for temporary food storage *(crop)*

Seagull

The gull is a bird that has mastered three different worlds. It can walk on land, swim on the sea and fly through the air. Gulls are large black, white and grey seabirds that usually live and nest near the coastline. They feed on live and dead prey that they find on the seashore or in the sea. The gull picks up this food – fish, shellfish and worms – using its strong beak. The hook at the end of the beak helps the bird keep a grip on its prey.

The gull has been able to master land, sea and air because of the special design of its feathers, bones, wings and feet. The feathers and bones are lightweight, which means that when flapping its wings the bird can lift itself off the ground. The feathers are also waterproof, so when the bird sits on water, it floats. The bird's slightly clawed feet can grip the ground as well as propel it through water. The webbing between the bird's claws acts in a similar way to flippers you might wear on your feet when swimming.

The upper and lower sections of the robot's beak are made of an inner framework (jawbones) *covered with an outer layer* (tough beak sheath).

Pike

A pike is a sleek and speedy, predatory fish that lives in freshwater rivers and lakes. When hunting, it hovers among water weeds until it sees a smaller fish swimming past. Then, with tremendous acceleration, it speeds forward to catch the fish in its sharp-toothed jaws.

The pike finds out where its prey is by using its large eyes, which look forward along grooves in the front part of the upper jaw. It can also sense water vibrations. These are picked up by a line of tiny openings along each side of the fish, called the lateral line. Minute sensors inside these openings can perceive very slight movements in the water and give clues about where the prey might be. A third sense used when catching prey is smell. The pike's forward-pointing nostrils pick up chemical clues from the surrounding waters.

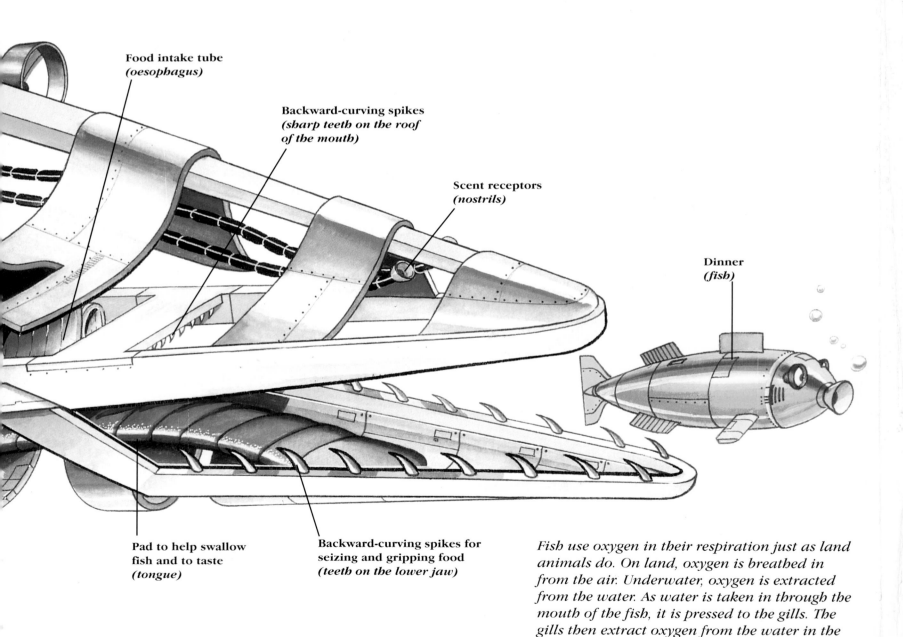

Food intake tube
(oesophagus)

Backward-curving spikes
(sharp teeth on the roof
of the mouth)

Scent receptors
(nostrils)

Dinner
(fish)

Pad to help swallow
fish and to taste
(tongue)

Backward-curving spikes for
seizing and gripping food
(teeth on the lower jaw)

Fish use oxygen in their respiration just as land animals do. On land, oxygen is breathed in from the air. Underwater, oxygen is extracted from the water. As water is taken in through the mouth of the fish, it is pressed to the gills. The gills then extract oxygen from the water in the same way that lungs take oxygen from the air.

34

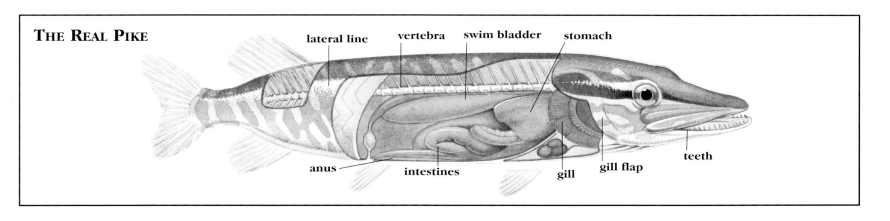

lateral line
vertebra
swim bladder
stomach

anus
intestines
gill
gill flap
teeth

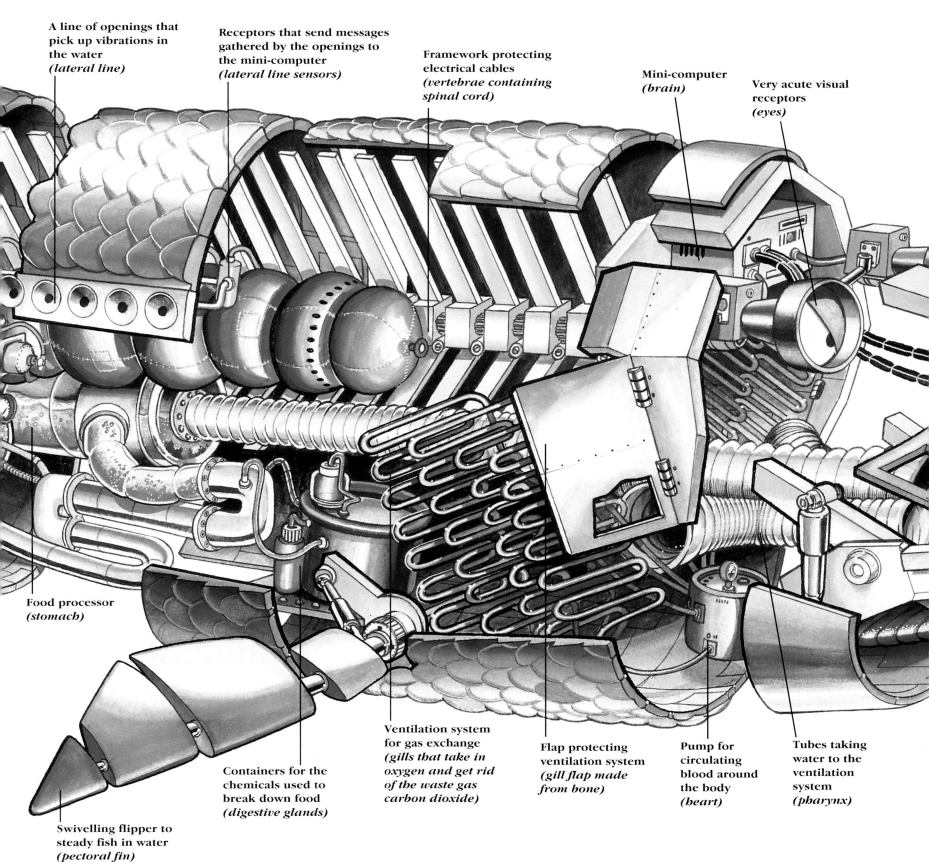

A line of openings that
pick up vibrations in
the water
(lateral line)

Receptors that send messages
gathered by the openings to
the mini-computer
(lateral line sensors)

Framework protecting
electrical cables
(vertebrae containing
spinal cord)

Mini-computer
(brain)

Very acute visual
receptors
(eyes)

Food processor
(stomach)

Swivelling flipper to
steady fish in water
(pectoral fin)

Containers for the
chemicals used to
break down food
(digestive glands)

Ventilation system
for gas exchange
(gills that take in
oxygen and get rid
of the waste gas
carbon dioxide)

Flap protecting
ventilation system
(gill flap made
from bone)

Pump for
circulating
blood around
the body
(heart)

Tubes taking
water to the
ventilation
system
(pharynx)

All birds have a special breathing system that allows them to take in a lot more oxygen through their lungs than mammals can. Air goes in through the windpipe, or trachea, to the lungs, and then out of the lungs to the air sacs. The air sacs act like bellows, alternately drawing air in and pushing it back out to the lungs, where more oxygen can be taken from it. This process gives the bird the energy it needs for flight.

Birds have digestive pouches that perform separate tasks. When the bird swallows a fish, the food goes down the oesophagus into the crop where it can be stored until the bird is ready to digest it. It will then go to the gizzard, which grinds it with stones that the bird has swallowed especially for this purpose. In the stomach and intestines, the nutrients are separated from the waste and distributed throughout the body.

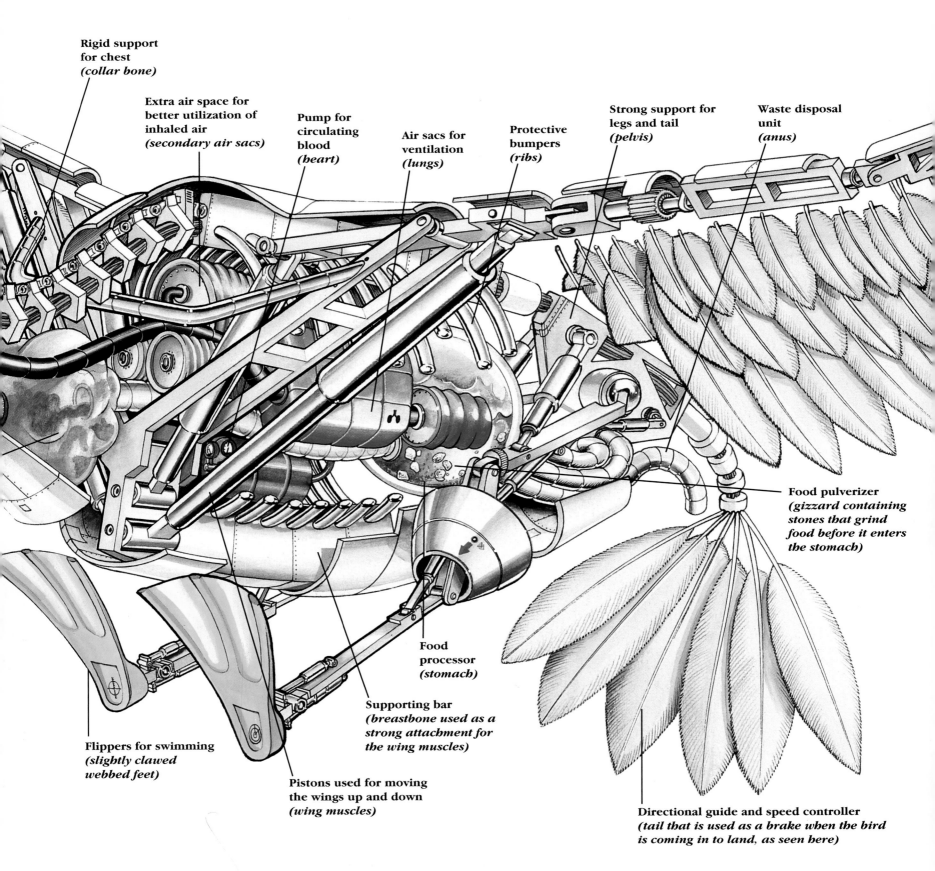

Rigid support for chest
(collar bone)

Extra air space for better utilization of inhaled air (secondary air sacs)

Pump for circulating blood (heart)

Air sacs for ventilation (lungs)

Protective bumpers (ribs)

Strong support for legs and tail (pelvis)

Waste disposal unit (anus)

Food pulverizer (gizzard containing stones that grind food before it enters the stomach)

Flippers for swimming (slightly clawed webbed feet)

Supporting bar (breastbone used as a strong attachment for the wing muscles)

Food processor (stomach)

Pistons used for moving the wings up and down (wing muscles)

Directional guide and speed controller (tail that is used as a brake when the bird is coming in to land, as seen here)

In the robot model, the leading edge of each wing is made of a long, hinged hollow spar (bone). Attached to this are rows of overlapping vanes (flight feathers) *that make up the main area of the wing. The wing structures provide lift and thrust for flight. They can be held out straight for gliding and soaring, or they can beat up and down, powered by huge flight pistons (flight muscles).*

GULL FACTS
Country: worldwide
Habitat: coastlines
Wingspan: 0.6–1.6 m (24–63 in)
Weight: up to about 2 kg (4½ lb)
Closest relative: albatross

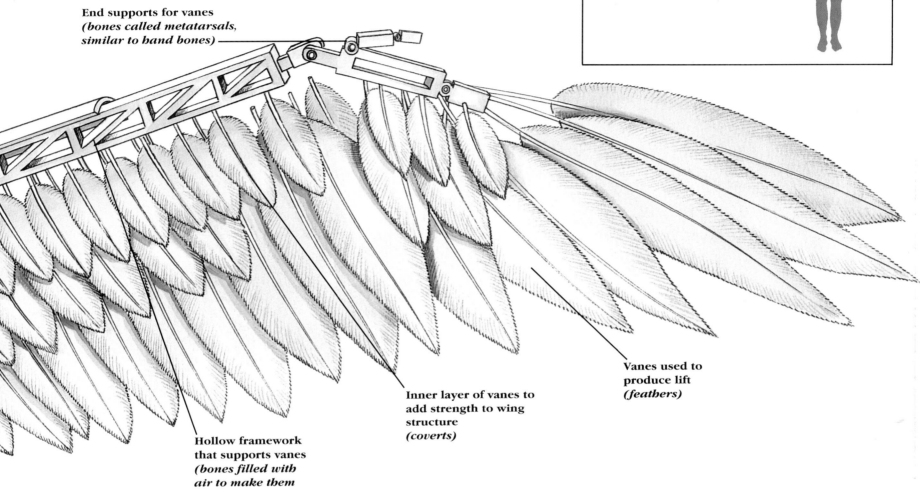

End supports for vanes *(bones called metatarsals, similar to hand bones)*

Inner layer of vanes to add strength to wing structure *(coverts)*

Vanes used to produce lift *(feathers)*

Hollow framework that supports vanes *(bones filled with air to make them light and strong)*

THE REAL GULL

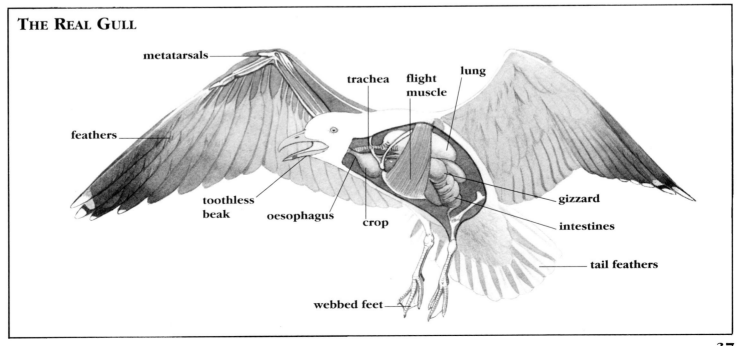

metatarsals

trachea

flight muscle

lung

feathers

toothless beak

oesophagus

crop

gizzard

intestines

tail feathers

webbed feet

As in the real animal, the robot's mouth is beak-shaped and toothless. The sharp edges of the beak are used to grab and cut up pieces of green grass or leaves that are then swallowed.

Protective helmet
(fused bones of the skull)

The tortoise's skull is made of strong bones that are fused together to make a tough, helmet-like casing. It shields the brain inside, just as the shell protects the animal's other soft organs.

Visual sensor
(eye)

Electrical fibres
(spinal cord inside spinal column)

Vents connected to the air intake pipe
(nostrils)

Tube to take food to processor
(oesophagus)

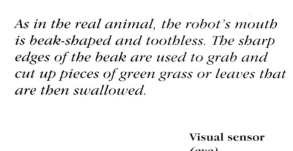

Tortoise

Built like an armoured car, the tortoise is a long-necked reptile. A reptile is a cold-blooded animal that lays eggs. Because it is cold-blooded, the tortoise has to live in warm climates, so that it never runs out of energy. If the weather became too cold, the tortoise would start to get sluggish because its body temperature would not be high enough for it to function properly.

Although tortoises may seem clumsy and slow, and therefore vulnerable, they can live for more than 70 years. In fact, the design of the tortoise has been so successful that the species has remained virtually unchanged for more than 65 million years.

Air intake pipe
(trachea, or windpipe)

THE REAL TORTOISE

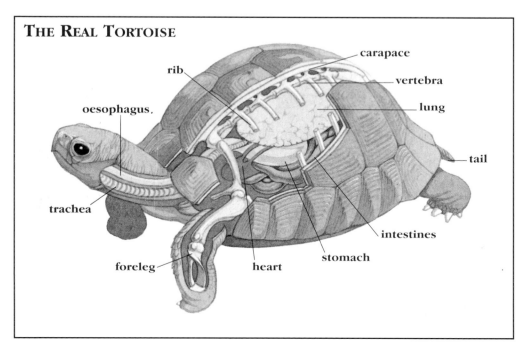

carapace

rib

vertebra

oesophagus

lung

trachea

tail

foreleg

heart

stomach

intestines

A hinged rod allows the robot's neck to be curved into an S bend so that it can be pulled back into the tortoise's armour. The legs and tail can also be pulled inside the shell, completely protecting all vulnerable parts of the tortoise's body. The skin around the neck, legs and tail folds up like an accordion and can easily squeeze into the small space inside the shell.

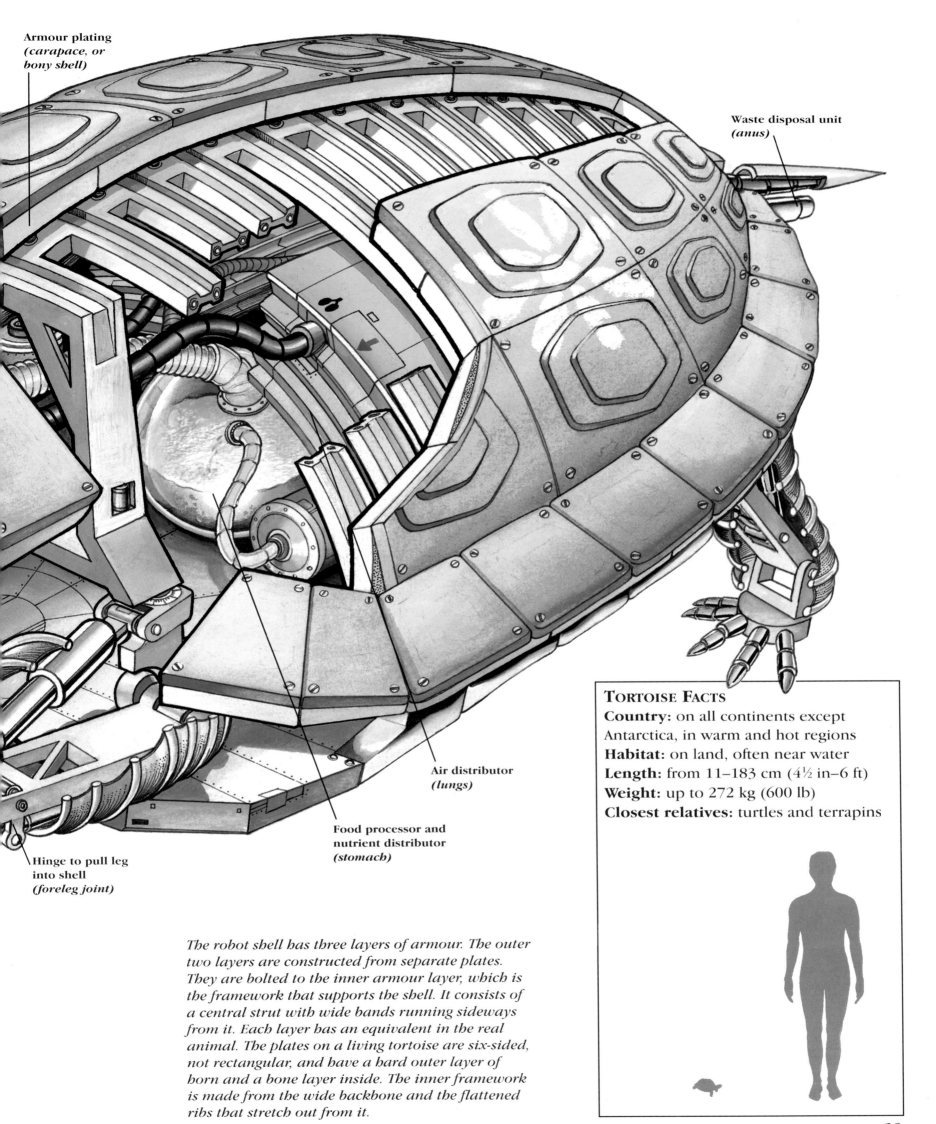

**Armour plating
(carapace, or
bony shell)**

**Waste disposal unit
(anus)**

**Air distributor
(lungs)**

**Food processor and
nutrient distributor
(stomach)**

**Hinge to pull leg
into shell
(foreleg joint)**

TORTOISE FACTS
Country: on all continents except
Antarctica, in warm and hot regions
Habitat: on land, often near water
Length: from 11–183 cm (4½ in–6 ft)
Weight: up to 272 kg (600 lb)
Closest relatives: turtles and terrapins

The robot shell has three layers of armour. The outer
two layers are constructed from separate plates.
They are bolted to the inner armour layer, which is
the framework that supports the shell. It consists of
a central strut with wide bands running sideways
from it. Each layer has an equivalent in the real
animal. The plates on a living tortoise are six-sided,
not rectangular, and have a hard outer layer of
horn and a bone layer inside. The inner framework
is made from the wide backbone and the flattened
ribs that stretch out from it.

Mussel

Mussels live on the seashore where saltwater tides go in and out. Between the high and low tide, you will find mussels by the thousands stuck tightly to rocks, harbour walls and wooden posts. When you come across them out of water, you will see only tightly-shut blue-black shells. The animal inside the shell cannot be seen. Only when the tide is in and the mussel is underwater does the animal inside show itself.

The mussel is a mollusc, which means it is grouped together with other animals that have soft bodies, usually covered with a hard shell. Snails and slugs are also molluscs. The mussel is a bivalve, which means the animal is surrounded by two connected shells.

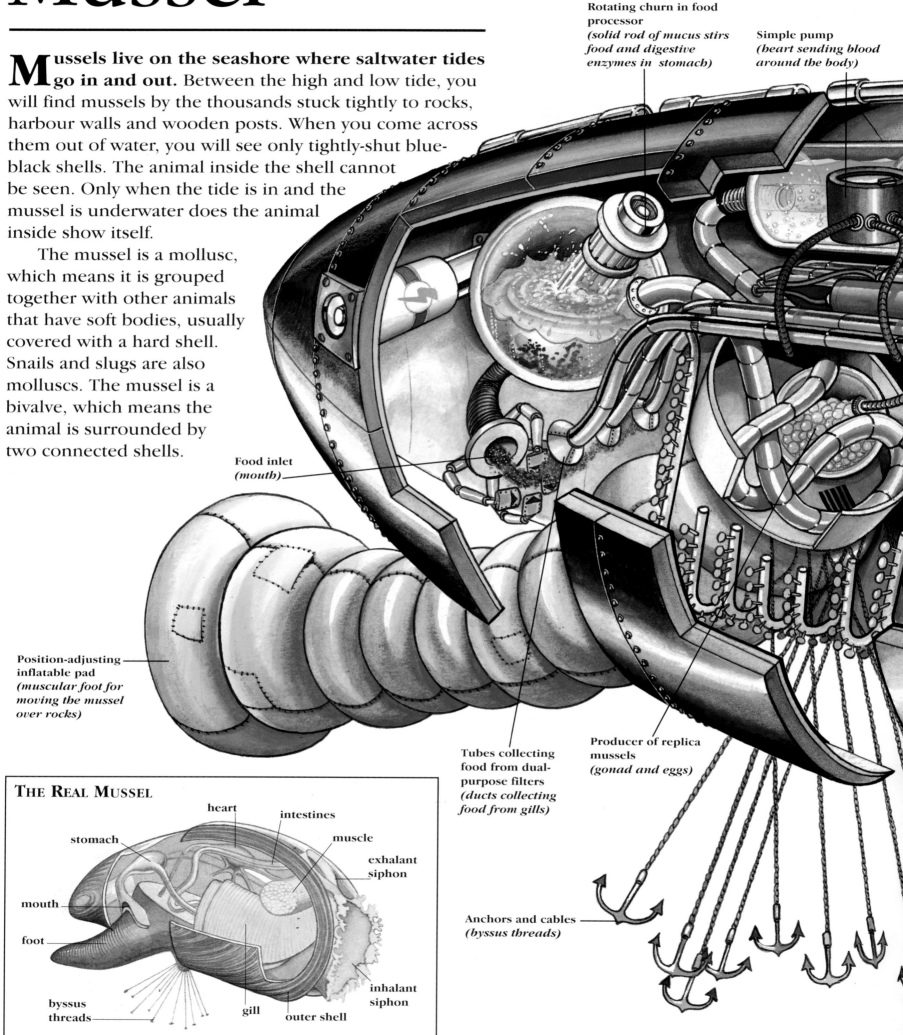

Rotating churn in food processor
(solid rod of mucus stirs food and digestive enzymes in stomach)

Simple pump
(heart sending blood around the body)

Food inlet
(mouth)

Position-adjusting inflatable pad
(muscular foot for moving the mussel over rocks)

Tubes collecting food from dual-purpose filters
(ducts collecting food from gills)

Producer of replica mussels
(gonad and eggs)

Anchors and cables
(byssus threads)

THE REAL MUSSEL

heart

intestines

muscle

exhalant siphon

stomach

mouth

foot

byssus threads

gill

outer shell

inhalant siphon

40

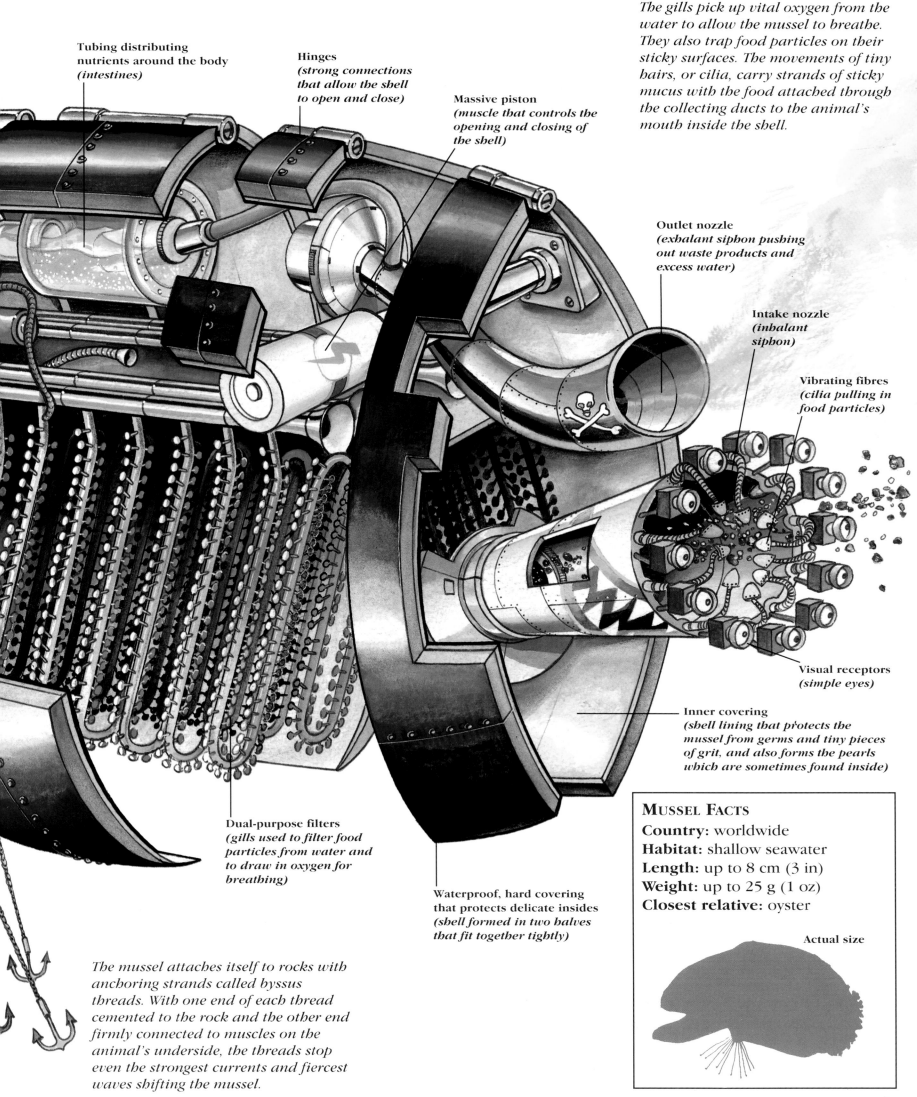

Tubing distributing nutrients around the body *(intestines)*

Hinges *(strong connections that allow the shell to open and close)*

Massive piston *(muscle that controls the opening and closing of the shell)*

The gills pick up vital oxygen from the water to allow the mussel to breathe. They also trap food particles on their sticky surfaces. The movements of tiny hairs, or cilia, carry strands of sticky mucus with the food attached through the collecting ducts to the animal's mouth inside the shell.

Outlet nozzle *(exhalant siphon pushing out waste products and excess water)*

Intake nozzle *(inhalant siphon)*

Vibrating fibres *(cilia pulling in food particles)*

Visual receptors *(simple eyes)*

Inner covering *(shell lining that protects the mussel from germs and tiny pieces of grit, and also forms the pearls which are sometimes found inside)*

Dual-purpose filters *(gills used to filter food particles from water and to draw in oxygen for breathing)*

Waterproof, hard covering that protects delicate insides *(shell formed in two halves that fit together tightly)*

The mussel attaches itself to rocks with anchoring strands called byssus threads. With one end of each thread cemented to the rock and the other end firmly connected to muscles on the animal's underside, the threads stop even the strongest currents and fiercest waves shifting the mussel.

MUSSEL FACTS
Country: worldwide
Habitat: shallow seawater
Length: up to 8 cm (3 in)
Weight: up to 25 g (1 oz)
Closest relative: oyster

Actual size

T4 Virus

Viruses are the smallest things that can be said to be living. You cannot see a virus with a normal microscope – it is only with a high-powered instrument called an electron microscope that scientists have been able to look at these amazingly small beings. It is difficult to imagine that viruses are alive because they do not feed or breathe. However, they do reproduce, which is what all living creatures do.

Viruses reproduce by attacking the smallest parts, or cells, of other living things. Each type of virus infects a different form of life. There are viruses, for example, that cause damage to mushrooms, and others that cause diseases in insects or in the plants that we grow as food. Many human diseases are the result of infections from viruses. Serious viral diseases include influenza, chicken pox and AIDS.

Viruses even attack bacteria, which are single-celled plants that can also cause diseases. The viruses that do this usually have tails which allow them to pierce through the outer covering of the bacterial cell, called the cell wall. One of the viruses that does this is the T4 virus.

A virus is always made up of two parts. The first part is a protective coat. The second, inside the coat, is a set of virus genes, making up a coiled string of DNA. Genes and DNA are the basic building blocks for all life. They control how all living things are put together.

A good way to think of what genes are is to liken DNA to a story. Every word of that story is a gene. If you put the words together in one order, they result in one particular story. Put them another way and the story changes. This is why there are so many different life forms. In the robot virus, the floppy discs are the words and the string of discs, the story.

Pirate flag
(this has no equivalent on the virus, but it shows that the virus robs from a bacterium and kills it!)

Floppy disc
(gene storing information about the make-up of the virus)

String of all the floppy discs together
(coiled DNA)

Strong outer layer
(protective coat arranged in six-sided shapes)

String of floppy discs ready to inject into target
(thread of DNA molecule ready to enter bacterium)

Extended spring
(outer coil that can squeeze up on landing)

Landing struts
(stabilizing legs)

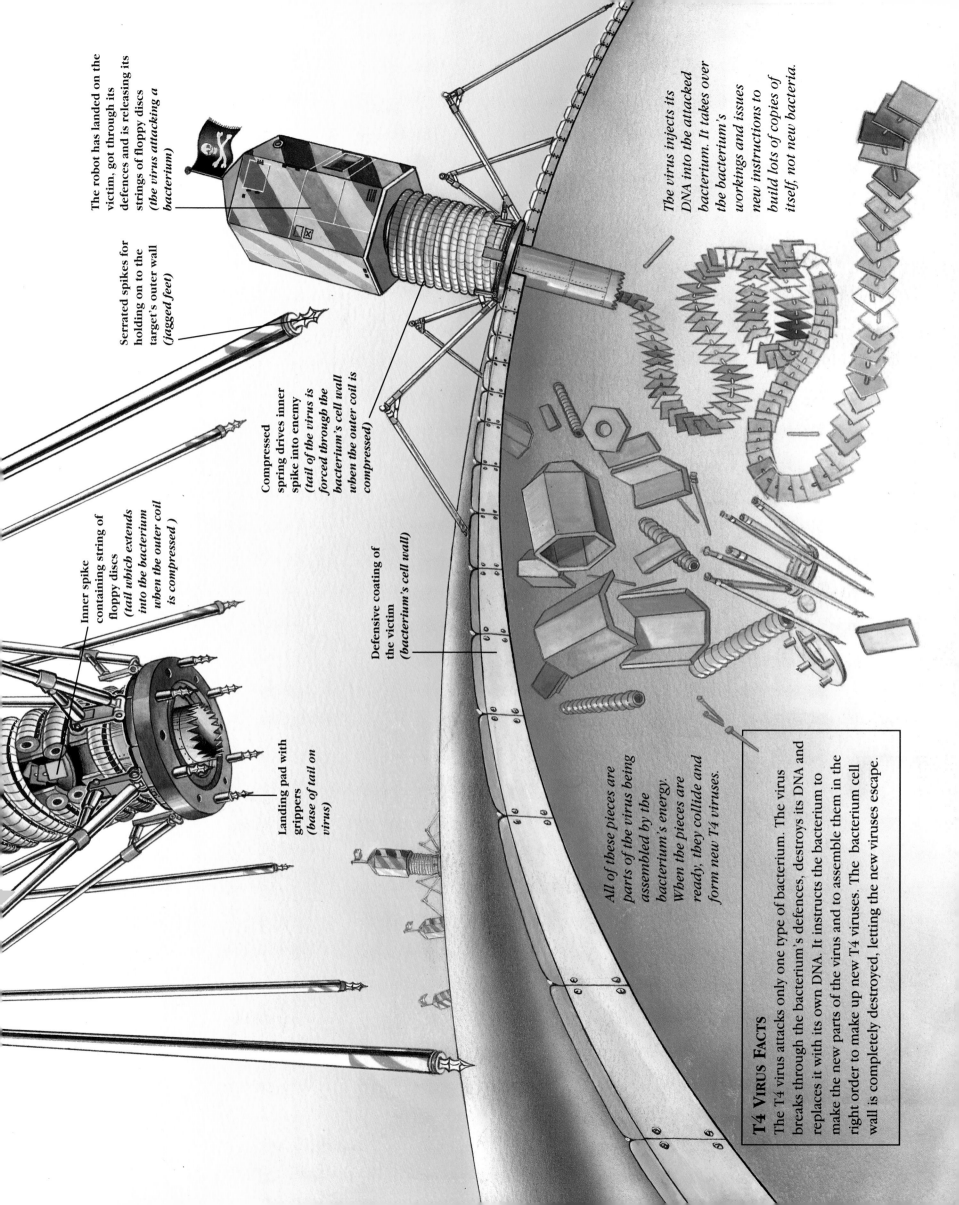

The robot has landed on the victim, got through its defences and is releasing its strings of floppy discs (*the virus attacking a bacterium*)

Serrated spikes for holding on to the target's outer wall (*jagged feet*)

Compressed spring drives inner spike into enemy (*tail of the virus is forced through the bacterium's cell wall when the outer coil is compressed*)

Inner spike containing string of floppy discs (*tail which extends into the bacterium when the outer coil is compressed*)

Landing pad with grippers (*base of tail on virus*)

Defensive coating of the victim (*bacterium's cell wall*)

The virus injects its DNA into the attacked bacterium. It takes over the bacterium's workings and issues new instructions to build lots of copies of itself, not new bacteria.

All of these pieces are parts of the virus being assembled by the bacterium's energy. When the pieces are ready, they collide and form new T4 viruses.

T4 Virus Facts
The T4 virus attacks only one type of bacterium. The virus breaks through the bacterium's defences, destroys its DNA and replaces it with its own DNA. It instructs the bacterium to make the new parts of the virus and to assemble them in the right order to make up new T4 viruses. The bacterium cell wall is completely destroyed, letting the new viruses escape.

GLOSSARY OF PARTS

Movement and Structure

All except the very smallest animals have bodies with some type of rigid skeleton. Movement occurs when muscles pull on the different parts of the skeleton. This happens when you walk, when a bird flies or when an ant carries a seed to its nest. Vertebrate animals have a skeleton made of bones inside their bodies, while invertebrates, such as insects, spiders and crabs, have a hard outer covering called an exoskeleton supporting their bodies.

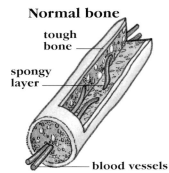

Normal bone
- tough bone
- spongy layer
- blood vessels

Stronger bone
- spongy layer
- tough bone
- blood vessels

Bones
All bones are made of a strong, rigid material. Each bone is a living organ with blood vessels in its centre. Usually the outer layers of the bone are dense, while the centre is more open and spongy. Where great support is needed, the outer layer is extra thick.

Bird bone
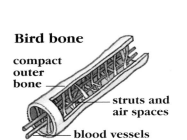
- compact outer bone
- struts and air spaces
- blood vessels

Bird bones
To fly, birds need light bodies. Their bones have a very thin outer layer. The inner spongy layer is made up of air-filled spaces between thin struts. This makes the bones very light.

Insect exoskeleton
The hard outer exoskeleton of an insect is called a cuticle. It is made of a horny material known as chitin. Each segment of an insect's body has a stiff cuticle, while the junctions between the segments are made of thinner, more flexible cuticle. Segments move when pairs of muscles that cross the junctions contract and release.

Insect leg
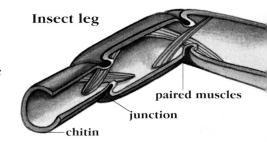
- chitin
- junction
- paired muscles

Hinges and joints
In vertebrates, joints are found where bones meet and movement occurs. Different joints allow different types of movement to happen.

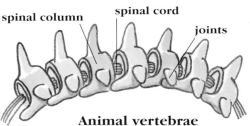

- hinges
- ball-and-socket joint
- flat joint

Joints
The elbow joint is like a hinge, while the shoulder joint, which can move in many directions, is a ball and socket joint. Flat joints, like those between the vertebrae, allow only a small range of movement.

Vertebrae
The backbone of a vertebrate is made up of a chain of small bones called vertebrae which are linked together to allow bending. The vertebrae protect the spinal cord, which lies in a canal in their centre. The robot vertebrae are constructed similarly.

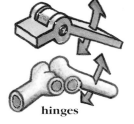

- spinal column
- spinal cord
- joints

Animal vertebrae

- framework
- joints
- fibres

Robot vertebrae

Muscles
Most animals move using muscles. Muscles are organs made of special fibres that have the power to contract (shorten by drawing together). When a muscle is stimulated by a nerve (*see* senses and nerves), it can change from a long, thin shape to a short, fat shape. Because the ends of the muscles are joined to different sections of the skeleton, the contracting muscles make the skeleton move. Some tubular organs, like the intestines, have layers of muscle fibres arranged in different directions. When these contract they push food through the organ.

Muscle fibre
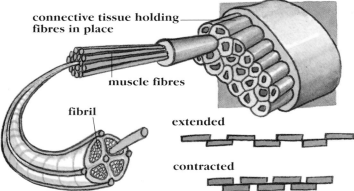
- connective tissue holding fibres in place
- muscle fibres
- fibril
- extended
- contracted

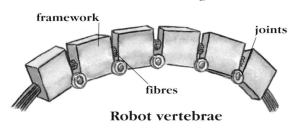
- longitudinal muscles
- circular muscles

Pistons
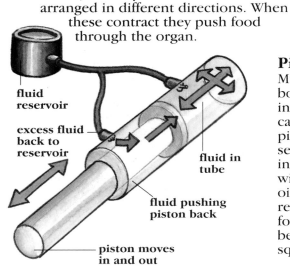
- fluid reservoir
- excess fluid back to reservoir
- fluid in tube
- fluid pushing piston back
- piston moves in and out

Muscles contract to move bones, whereas the pistons in the robots push out to cause movement. Each piston fits tightly inside a second tube. The space inside the tube is filled with fluid, usually a special oil. When fluid from a reservoir enters the tube, it forces the piston out because liquids cannot be squeezed or compressed.

Muscular limbs
The tentacles of the giant squid have no bones. For movement, they use a system of longitudinal and circular muscles. The robot's system shows how these work. On one side of the tube the wires contract and squeeze the discs close together, pulling the tube in that direction. To straighten the tube out, wires contract on the opposite side.

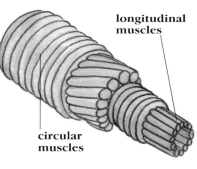
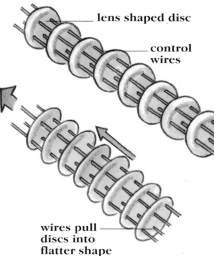
- lens shaped disc
- control wires
- wires pull discs into flatter shape

Feathers

Feathers are made of the tough substance keratin. Each feather has a central shaft called a rachis from which extend thin side pieces called barbs. Tiny branches on the barbs, the barbules, allow the barbs to lock flexibly together and form the vanes of the feather. If the barbs of a vane split apart, all the bird has to do is pull the feather through its beak and the barbules will link together again.

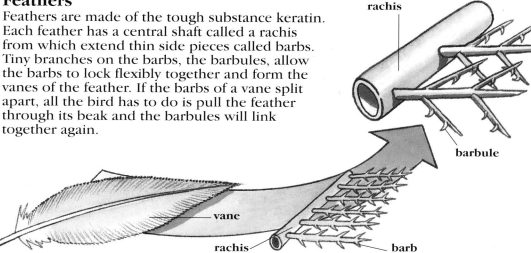

rachis

barbule

vane

rachis

barb

Scales

A reptile's scale consists of a flap of tough keratin. Between each scale and the next lies a more flexible, thinner layer of keratin. Together the scales act like chain-mail armour and protect the reptile. Under the keratin layer of the scales are pigment cells that give the reptile its colour.

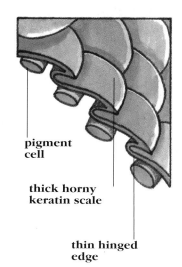

pigment cell

thick horny keratin scale

thin hinged edge

Senses and Nerves

Most animals control their actions with a nervous system. This is made up of a brain and nerves that connect the brain to different parts of the body. The animal's senses receive and pass information about the outside world to the brain. The brain analyses this data and sends messages to different parts of the body, causing them to react. The brain also has memory stores so that past experience can be used to influence future behaviour. Most insects have no brain, but instead have groups of nerve cells, called ganglia, which act in a similar way to a brain.

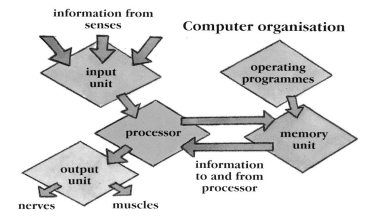

information from senses

Computer organisation

input unit

operating programmes

processor

memory unit

output unit

information to and from processor

nerves

muscles

Computers

The robots' brains are computers. Information is gathered from the sensors of the robots. Output signals travel along fibres to make parts of the robot work. The processing unit of the computer operates programmes that are used to make decisions. The computer also has a large memory bank, in which data is stored.

Nerves and cables

Signals in a nervous system and in a computer are both electrical. In a nervous system, the signals pass between nerve cells along paths called axons. In a computer, the signals consist of electrical currents that travel along very thin wires.

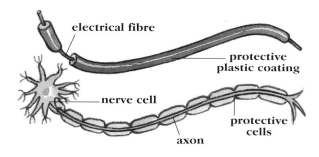

electrical fibre

protective plastic coating

nerve cell

axon

protective cells

Insect touch

The cuticle of an insect has sensory hairs extending from it. Each hair can bend at its base. If the hair senses something, it bends easily and a sensory cell sends an impulse to the ganglia. This is the basis for the insect's sense of touch.

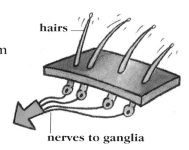

hairs

nerves to ganglia

Hearing and vibration sense

Animals usually have special sensory organs that allow them to receive sound waves. The system for hearing is similar in all animals. The sound waves hit a membrane which vibrates. The vibrations are passed through a fluid to nerve cells. These send signals to the brain, which are interpreted as sound. Insects' ears can be anywhere on their body. A fish's lateral line has no membrane but fluid passes on vibrations to the sense cells.

Insect's ear

nerves to brain

sense cells

tympanic membrane

sound waves

Ears and acoustic receptors

Land vertebrates have two ears. Sound makes the ear drum membrane, tiny bones and fluid vibrate. A fish picks up vibrations through its lateral line. Sensory cells send messages to the fish's brain. An acoustic receptor in a robot does much the same thing, but it has a diaphragm that vibrates and passes signals on to an amplifier.

nerves to brain

cochlea fluid

Mammal's ear

ear bones

ear drum

sound waves

Fish's lateral line

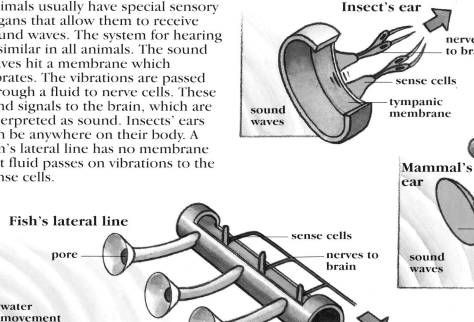

sense cells

nerves to brain

pore

water movement

Acoustic receptor

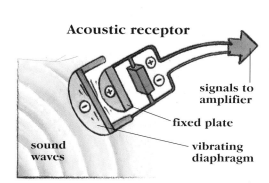

signals to amplifier

fixed plate

vibrating diaphragm

sound waves

Seeing

Most animals have eyes. There are two major types of eyes. The one found in vertebrates is a fluid-filled sphere with a transparent window, or cornea, at the front. Light passes through the cornea and is focused by a lens to form an image on a light-sensitive surface called the retina. The retina is made up of millions of tiny light-sensitive cells called rods and cones. These convert the image on the retina into a pattern of nerve impulses that are sent to the brain to be interpreted.

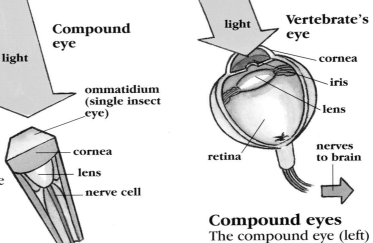

Compound eye

light

ommatidium (single insect eye)

cornea

lens

nerve cell

nerve to brain

Vertebrate's eye

light

cornea

iris

lens

retina

nerves to brain

Visual receptors

Visual receptors, such as video cameras, have lens systems that focus an image on the back of a light-proof box. Sensory systems at the back of the box convert the image into electrical signals that transmit the image to the computer.

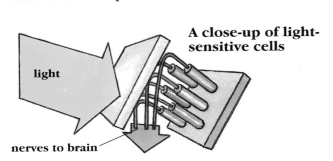

A close-up of light-sensitive cells

light

nerves to brain

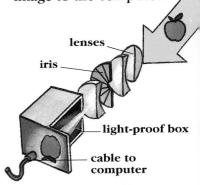

lenses

iris

light-proof box

cable to computer

Compound eyes

The compound eye (left) is found in invertebrates, such as insects. It is made up of hundreds, or even thousands, of tiny, telescope-like sensor units, called ommatidia. Each of these responds to light that passes down its length.

Sense of smell

In the nasal passages of vertebrates are cells that respond to all sorts of chemical substances in the air. The nerve signals that these cells produce provide the animal with a sense of smell. Different cells recognize different scents. The clues that a sense of smell provides enable animals to find food, escape from predators and find mates.

nasal passage

smell substances

air in nostril

nerve signal to brain

sensory cells

Respiration and Digestion

Animals need energy. This comes from the food they eat. Food is digested and passed into the bloodstream as tiny particles of nutrients. These are then absorbed into cells. The nutrients are broken down when they combine with oxygen. When this breakdown (internal respiration) happens, large amounts of energy are released and the waste gas carbon dioxide is produced.

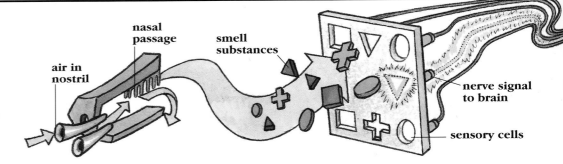

energy

nutrients

cell

water

oxygen

carbon dioxide

Breathing

For nutrients to be broken down, an animal needs a constant supply of oxygen. Land animals get their oxygen from the air. Animals that live underwater get oxygen from the water. Land and water animals breathe to get the oxygen, and the breathing is called external respiration.

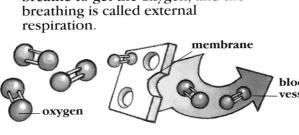

membrane

oxygen

blood vessel

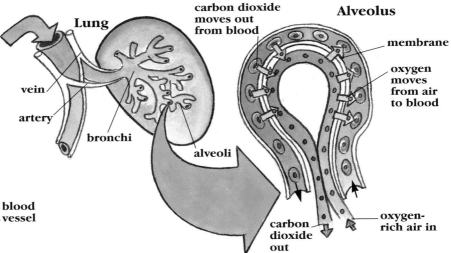

Lung

carbon dioxide moves out from blood

Alveolus

membrane

oxygen moves from air to blood

vein

artery

bronchi

alveoli

carbon dioxide out

oxygen-rich air in

Lungs

Land animals pull oxygen into their lungs by breathing. The inner lining of the lungs is a huge, moist surface covered with tiny blood vessels called capillaries. Blood passing through these vessels picks up the oxygen as it travels across the very thin membrane that divides the air from the blood (far left).

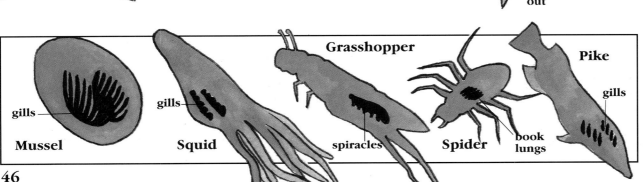

Grasshopper

Pike

gills

Mussel

gills

Squid

spiracles

Spider

book lungs

gills

Other types

Insects and fish have a wide variety of oxygen-gathering organs. Most of the aquatic animals have gills. Water flows across gills, so that the blood vessels inside can pick up oxygen. Insects and spiders have a series of tubes that lead to the inner respiratory organs.

Blood supply

Blood is a body fluid which has many functions. It carries oxygen and energy-rich nutrients to all of the body cells for internal respiration. It removes waste substances, like carbon dioxide and urea, from the body cells and carries them to the lungs and kidneys to be expelled. It also carries hormones around the body. Hormones are special substances that control some of the body's activities. The hormone insulin, for example, controls the levels of sugars in the blood.

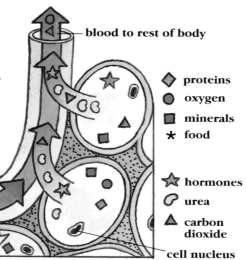

blood to rest of body

◇ proteins
○ oxygen
■ minerals
✳ food

☆ hormones
✐ urea
△ carbon dioxide

cell nucleus

Simple hearts

A heart is a muscle in the system of tubes, blood vessels, that passes blood around an animal's body. By pumping, the heart pushes blood through the body. This pumping action is caused by muscles in the wall of the heart. In insects and molluscs, the heart is not much more than thickened blood vessels. Muscles squeeze around the vessels to force blood through the body.

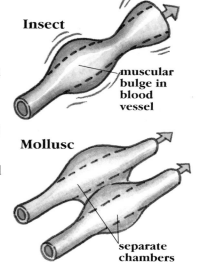

Insect

muscular bulge in blood vessel

Mollusc

separate chambers

Pumps

The hearts of animals use muscles to push blood through the vessels in the blood system. In the robots, a variety of pumping machines are used to move body fluids. The rotor pump (left) uses spinning rotor blades to push the fluid through an outlet tube.

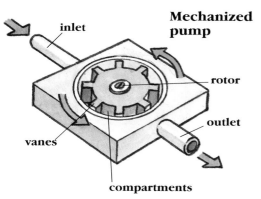

Mechanized pump

inlet

rotor

outlet

vanes

compartments

Circulation

In insects, blood travels from the heart to the body where it picks up oxygen. In fish, blood circulates from the heart to the gills, through the body, and back to the heart. In land vertebrates, blood travels from the heart to the lungs, back to the heart, and then into the body before returning to the heart.

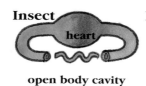

Insect

heart

open body cavity

Fish

body

gills

heart

lungs

oxygen in blood

heart

carbon dioxide in blood

body

Mammal

Digestion

This is the chemical process that breaks food down into nutrients, which the body uses for energy. Digestion begins when food is chewed by the teeth. The process continues with the help of digestive enzymes. These substances break down particles of food into smaller ones that can be absorbed by cells. Proteins are turned into amino acids, starches into sugars and fats into fatty acids.

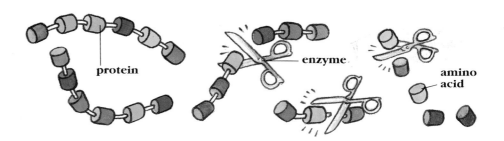

protein

enzyme

amino acid

The process

All except a few tiny animals have an intestine. In mammals, food is first mixed with saliva in the mouth, which lubricates its passage and adds digestive enzymes. These begin to break the food down. In the stomach, acid that kills bacteria is added, and more digestive enzymes are secreted from the stomach wall. In the intestines, additional enzymes from the pancreas and liver continue the process of digestion. The nutrients that are produced are absorbed through the wall of the intestine. The final sections of the intestine remove excess water from the material that remains. This waste, called faeces, is then expelled through the anus.

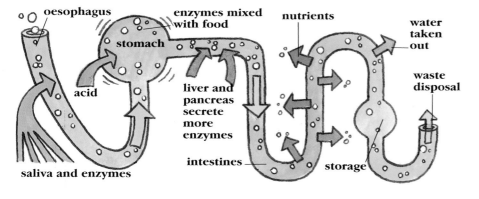

oesophagus

enzymes mixed with food

stomach

acid

nutrients

water taken out

waste disposal

liver and pancreas secrete more enzymes

intestines

storage

saliva and enzymes

Digestive organs

All these animals have similar digestive organs. They follow the same system as described above. But there are some differences. The giraffe has a stomach with four chambers that help digest grass. The bird, grasshopper and chameleon have food storage areas called crops. The mussel has a mouth inside its shell, which collects food particles gathered by its gills.

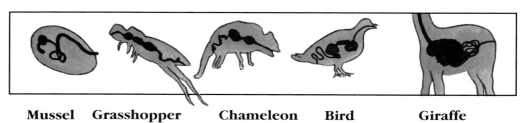

Mussel   Grasshopper   Chameleon   Bird   Giraffe

Index

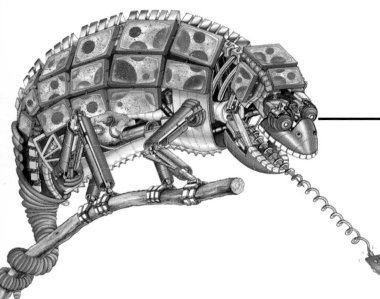

The numbers in *italics* refer to illustrations of the real animals.

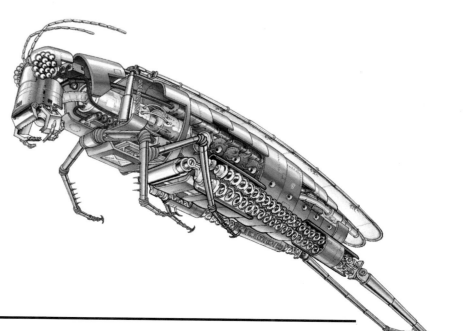

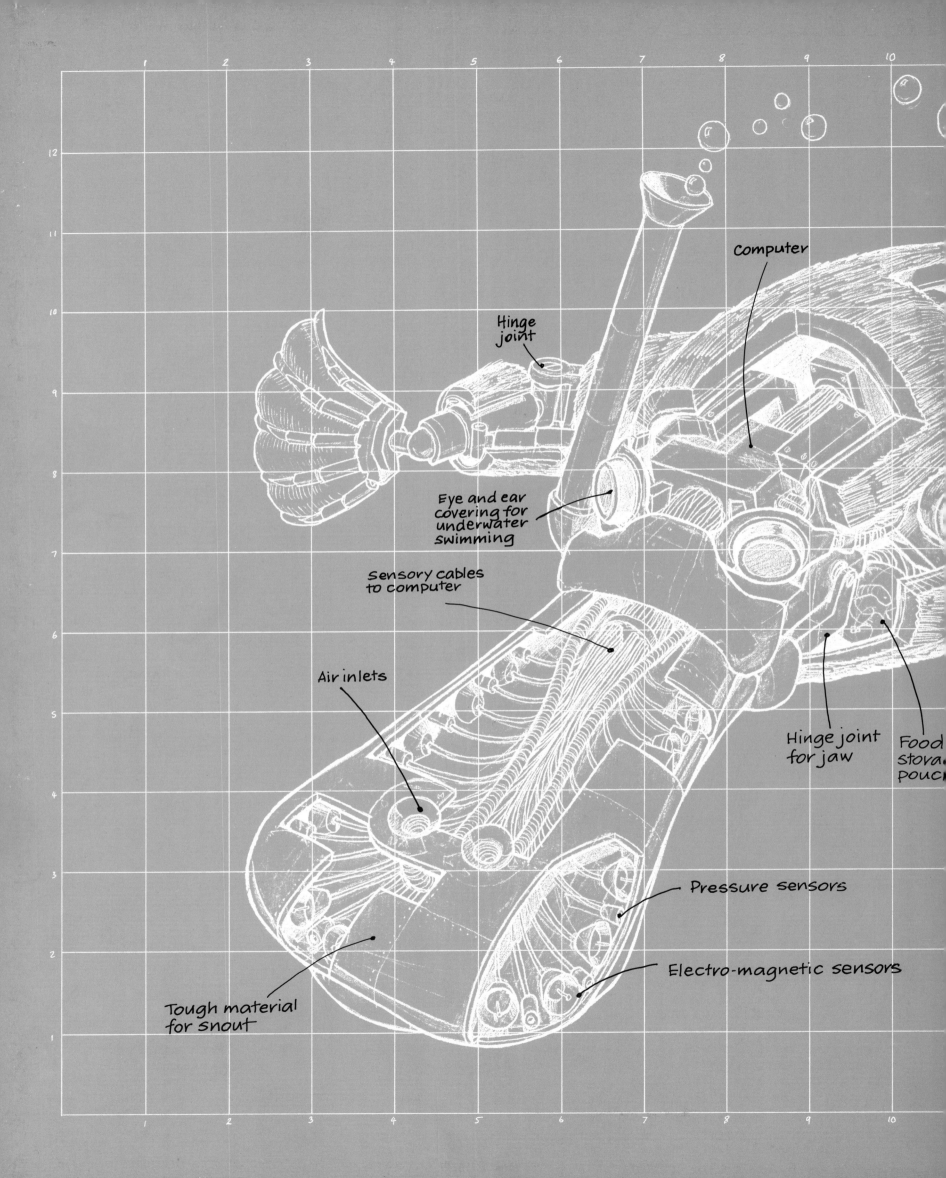

Computer

Hinge joint

Eye and ear covering for underwater swimming

Sensory cables to computer

Air inlets

Hinge joint for jaw

Food storage pouch

Pressure sensors

Electro-magnetic sensors

Tough material for snout